Intercultural Empathetic Competent Teaching

Alia Ballita

First published by Busybird Publishing 2023

Copyright © 2023 Alia Ballita

ISBN
Print: 978-1-922954-56-5
Ebook: 978-1-922954-57-2

This work is copyright. Apart from any use permitted under the *Copyright Act 1968*, no part of this publication may be reproduced, stored in a retrieval system or transmitted in any form or by any means, electronic, mechanical, photocopying, recording or otherwise, without the prior written permission of Alia Ballita.

The information in this book is based on the author's experiences and opinions. The author and publisher disclaim responsibility for any adverse consequences, which may result from use of the information contained herein. Permission to use any external content has been sought by the author. Any breaches will be rectified in further editions of the book.

Cover Image: Kev Howlett @ Busybird Publishing
Cover design: Kev Howlett @ Busybird Publishing
Layout and typesetting: Sarah Neilsen @ Busybird Publishing

Busybird Publishing
2/118 Para Road
Montmorency, Victoria
Australia 3094
www.busybird.com.au

Contents

Background Chapter — 1
    Critical Self-Reflection on Race and Culture — 1
    Race, Culture, and the Adaptive Unconsciousness — 3
    Culture, Race and Ethnicity: A Complicated Relationship — 6
    Ethnic Group — 8
    Intergroup Attitudes in Primary School Children — 12
    Racism, Education and Academic Outcomes — 13
    Educational Policies in Australia — 17
    Educational practice in Australia — 20

1 - Motivation, Approaches to Learning, and Retelling — 23
    Motivation to Learning — 24
    Approaches to Learning — 31
    Retelling Story as an imaginative approach to enhance Indigenous Australian Children — 39

2 - Multicultural Education in Australia and Victoria — 55
    Australian Context — 56
    Multicultural Education — 57
    The Implementation of Multicultural Education — 59
    Multicultural Education in Australia — 61
    Multicultural Education in Victoria/Australia — 62
    Australian/Victorian Students with Extensive Support Needs — 64

3 - Cultural Competence	67
Cultural Competence	68
1 - Multicultural Knowledge	75
2 - Attitudes Towards Cultural Differences	76
3 - Cross-Cultural Skills	78
4 - Multicultural Awareness	79
Multicultural Competence in Australia	80
Intercultural Awareness vs. Intercultural Empathy	90
4 - Teachers' Intercultural Competence	**91**
Teachers' Intercultural Competence	96
The Importance of Interculturally Competent Teachers	97
Teacher Training in Intercultural Education	99
Teacher Continuous Professional Development for Inclusion	100
Frameworks for Teacher Competency	104
Developing Disciplinary Literacy in Pre-Service Teachers	106
The Need for Teacher Training in Australia	108
5 - Significance of Empathy in Education	**111**
Empathy	112
Types of Empathy	114
Benefits of Empathy	115
Teachers' Empathy	118
Incorporating Empathy into Education and Teaching	119
Conceptualizing Empathy	120
Knowing from a Personal Perspective	121

6 - Intercultural Empathetic Competence — **123**

Significance of Empathy to Intercultural
Classroom Practice — 124

The Epistemology of Empathy — 126

Empathy as Social Necessity. — 127

Empathy and Discomfort as Pedagogies in
Multicultural Teacher Education — 128

Cultural/Intercultural Empathy — 129

Previous Research on Ethnocultural Empathy — 132

Teaching and Disciplining with Empathy — 135

Teachers Need to Act Interculturally Empathetically — 136

References — 140

Background Chapter

This chapter provides an overview of the place of anti-racism education and intercultural education within international conventions and Australia's national educational policy as well as the educational practices in Australia.

Critical Self-Reflection on Race and Culture

One of the most fundamental elements of cultural competence is the development of ongoing critical self-reflection. Critical self-reflection on race and culture within a diverse cultural context requires education practitioners and researchers to engage in one of the most difficult processes for all individuals: honest self-assessment, critique, and evaluation of one's own thoughts, behaviours, cultural patterns, methods of expression, and cultural knowledge and ways of being. Critical reflection and self-assessment draw on one's ability to seek deeper levels of self-knowledge and to acknowledge how one's own worldview shapes one's perspectives and beliefs about oneself as well as one's students, their families, and their communities.

The formation of a critical reflection paradigm is extremely difficult, if not impossible, without honest and sustained self-reflection. Critical reflection can be difficult because it forces individuals to ask challenging questions related to their construction of individuals from diverse racial, ethnic, and cultural backgrounds.

Critical self-reflection may be more difficult for some White teachers because race is not often spoken about by those from racially privileged or dominant positions. G. R. Howard (2006) talks about the salience of White dominance and how "most White educators want schooling to become more than a mechanism of social control that favours White children" (p. 51), and strongly advocates the importance of self-examination to disrupt racially favourable beliefs toward Whites.

Sleeter (2008) found that White teachers generally resist examining long-held beliefs and "bring little awareness or understanding of discrimination, especially racism [and], are not aware of how racism works in schools and society" and about "how it is reproduced daily" (p. 560). Moreover, she asserts that these teachers typically "bring virtually no conceptual framework for understanding visible inequalities rather than the dominant deficit framework . . . [are] generally ignorant of communities of colour, fear them and fear discussing race and racism," and "lack awareness of themselves as cultural beings" (p. 560).

Race, Culture, and the Adaptive Unconsciousness

There is a growing body of evidence to support the prevalence of Racism in Australia and internationally according to Baron and Banaji (2006). Research examining intergroup attitudes and racial bias in children has also predominantly been conducted internationally, particularly in the UK and North America (Baron and Banaji 2006). But more research is needed with younger children, particularly in an Australian primary school context. This is especially important to examine in young children given that research indicates prejudice has the potential to develop in the beginning years of school.

The risks associated with racism and racial bias, and the subsequent outcomes that this has on children and the overall school culture are substantial. Anti-racist education holds the potential to truly reflect the cultural hybridity of our diverse, multi-cultural society through the canons of knowledge that educators celebrate, proffer, and embody. Therefore, it is important to examine the ways in which this may be minimised (Yared, Grové and Chapman, 2020b).

One of the most painful parts of the critical reflection process entails acknowledging or recognizing one's own privilege as a member of a group that has received unearned opportunity and advantage.

What is crucial about acknowledging privilege is that failure to begin dismantling these privileges once the individual becomes conscious of them is, in many ways, tantamount to acting in discriminatory ways. Therefore, it is not enough for the individual to say, "I have privilege because of my racial membership," but she must take active steps to ensure that future actions do not reinforce the remnants of that privilege.

Perhaps the most important aspect of developing cultural competence, critical reflection, and the adaptive unconscious, and of dismantling privilege, is to recognize that neutrality is equivalent to acting against equity, fairness, and justice in the classroom. Teaching is always a political act that is never neutral. Failure to recognize the complexities of action and neutrality can result in strained relationships between teachers and students from culturally diverse groups.

An essential aspect of culturally competent teaching is the willingness of the educator to examine his or her own ways of knowing, sources of information, and value-laden perspectives, and then to be willing to acknowledge the fact that students frequently bring their own unique skill sets and knowledge bases to the classroom.

Teachers can work toward the establishment of a relationship that is undergirded by a mutual respect of the positionality of the teacher and the learner in a way that promotes reciprocal teaching and learning of content across different contexts. Essential to this stance of cultural competence is the way it can enhance all aspects of the learning environment.

Teel and Obidah (2008) contend that cultural competence is "as important as competence in classroom management, curriculum, lesson planning and delivery, and assessment . . . all those competencies become stronger and stronger as a teacher becomes more and more racially and culturally competent" (p. 3). Cross and colleagues (1989) stress the importance of cultural competence because it implies having the capacity to function within the context of culturally integrated patterns of human behaviour defined by a group.

Educating students in their own cultural context can include structuring instruction, content, and assessment in ways that are tied to students' lived experiences, personal background, or cultural ways of knowing and being (American, 2022). Issues of cultural competence and racial awareness are not restricted to the work of practitioners and school leaders, but have equal relevance to researchers engaged in documenting, describing, and evaluating the lived experiences of people from different backgrounds. Teachers have a tremendous responsibility and obligation to earn the trust of students from diverse backgrounds. It is vital for members of racially privileged groups to not merely provide lip service to the wrongs of racism and racial oppression and discrimination, but to consistently speak out against and raise objections to them, while continually acting in ways that move us toward racial and cultural equity.

Within the context of schools, cultural competence and racial awareness may entail educators advocating on behalf of students if colleagues make disparaging comments about them, their families, or their intellectual abilities. Cultural practices that various students may express, such as religious traditions (e.g., Ramadan with fasting and prayer rituals or Jehovah's Witness practices of not pledging allegiance to the flag), should be acknowledged as different and not as deficient.

Culture, Race and Ethnicity: A Complicated Relationship

To understand racial issues in education, an understanding of the interconnectedness between race, ethnicity and culture is necessary. When considering these constructs, there is debate in the field around whether they are distinct, interlinked, or some variation in between. Culture is something we learn from our environment, and it contributes to a collective mindset that differentiates one group of people from another while ethnicity has been somewhat socially constructed, it also has genetic markers; race however does not and is instead considered to be a socially constructed category.

For some individuals, culture, race, and ethnicity overlap. However, recent research has questioned whether the assumption of these constructs being inherently linked, is a biased assumption that researchers should be mindful of. There has been a tendency in research to assume racially minoritized groups are influenced strongly by cultural factors, whereas white indivicuals are shaped predominantly by psychological factors (e.g., personality).

Moreover, there is a visibility when it comes to race and ethnicity that is more prominent than it is for culture, religion, or language. One can, to an extent, hide or minimise the visibility of their culture, religion, or language so that it is not immediately obvious (e.g., by removing religious symbols from clothing). That same individual cannot hide the visibility of their race with the same ease (e.g., skin colour or facial features). In addition, research has shown that the development of bias is not strictly universal, and people often express different forms of bias in different ways and to varying degrees.

Moreover, different forms of bias and prejudice may present differently across the lifespan (Baron and Banaji 2006). This may be true for the way in which racial bias and racism manifests, compared to closely linked biases such as religious or cultural bias. This is particularly important given some research has indicated children, especially younger children, may rely on visual cues to guide their intergroup attitudes and behaviours (e.g., skin colour or visible religious items).

Australia shares many cultural similarities with other western nations such as the US, the UK and Canada. However, many differences also exist that may influence the generalisability of international research to an Australian context. This impedes our understanding of racism and racial bias in Australian schools, subsequently impeding our ability to combat these issues adequately.

Ethnic Group

According to Australian Census 2006, Victoria is a multicultural society comprising people from more than 200 nations, speaking more than 200 languages and dialects, and following more than 120 faiths. Multicultural education is not a mainstream issue in Australia. Australian classrooms are full of children from a range of cultural backgrounds and the aim of the government is to bring about integration of students from different cultural backgrounds and provide equal educational opportunities for all of them.

However, there are ethnic group differences in academic achievement among Australian students, with

Aboriginal students performing substantially below and Asian students above their peers.

One factor that may contribute to these effects is societal stereotypes of Australian Asian and Aboriginal students, which may bias teachers' evaluations and influence student outcomes (Dandy et al., 2015). Australian Asian and Aboriginal stereotypes may impact teacher evaluations and student outcomes in part due to societal stereotypes (Dandy et al., 2015).

Academic achievement among Australian students varies by ethnic group. Aboriginal Australian students perform below their peers in school. Children from Aboriginal Australian families are less likely to attend school and remain in school. Therefore, the risk of having to repeat a year in early primary schooling is high. In addition, they are overrepresented in special education referrals. As a result, many Indigenous students seem to be caught between long-established racism and a new 'hunt for disabilities' in school settings (Dandy et al., 2015).

Hence, there is now growing evidence of ethnic group differences in academic achievement among Australian students. It is well documented that Aboriginal Australian students lag their peers in terms of school performance. Aboriginal Australian children have lower school participation and retention rates are at greater risk of being required to repeat a year in early primary schooling and are substantially over-represented in referrals to special education.

Relatively less is known about the school performance of other Australian ethnic minorities, although there is some evidence that students from Asian backgrounds outperform other groups. Whilst researchers have proposed several explanations for these ethnic group differences in achievement, particularly regarding the poor performance of Aboriginal Australian students, surprisingly the roles of societal stereotypes and teacher expectations have been relatively unexplored.

A recent OECD (2018) study found inequity in Australian education was a major issue. The Programme for International Student Assessment (PISA) report said disparities in student performance relating to their socio-economic status started at an early age and widened throughout their lives. The report concluded "upward educational and social mobility" would be boosted if gaps relating to students' socio-economic status during schooling were reduced.

Likewise, a recent UNICEF Office of Research study found Australian schools had one of the biggest performance gaps between top and bottom ranked students in the wealthier parts of the world. Equity is essential because education is fundamental to the wellbeing and development of individuals and society. Getting the best out of our children leads to significant economic benefits.

With many academic studies finding equity is a notable predictor to how people perform when they leave school in the areas of employment, financial security, health, well-being and civic participation (Equity in Australian Education / Gonski Institute for Education - UNSW Sydney).

However, if equity in education was boosted across the nation's schools, the performance of underachieving students would be significantly improved, with more students from low socio-economic backgrounds achieving academic success.

Despite attempts to create standards for vocational education and training (VET) teachers, nothing that systematically addresses VET teaching performance has emerged. The creation of a national set of standards is complicated by the fact that the VET system in Australia (as in many other countries) has responsibilities carried out at both Federal and State levels. No move in this direction has been undertaken by the Federal government, and state-government initiatives, such as in Queensland and Victoria have so far not been formally endorsed.

The nearest to a national (but not government-endorsed) set of standards is the 'VET Practitioner Capability Framework' (Innovations & Business Skills Australia [IBSA], n.d.) developed by the former Skills Council responsible for the Training and Education Training Package (Smith and Yasukawa, 2017).

Intergroup Attitudes in Primary School Children

There is a connection between children's attitudes regarding race and the attitudes of their teachers. In relation to race, a child's primary school years are a pivotal stage in their social cognitive development (Rutland and Killen 2015). It is a time where children begin to understand the world around them and their place within it.

Racial bias and racism evident in adults do not manifest in adulthood. It begins in childhood, slowly develops across the lifespan, becoming deeply ingrained and resistant to change by adulthood (Rutland and Killen 2015). Prejudice emerges simultaneously as children's social-cognitive ability is developing (Aboud et al. 2012). Just as a child's negative views regarding race and ethnicity develop, so do their prosocial attitudes (Rutland and Killen 2015) and their sense of morality. Additionally, despite explicit racial bias seeming to become more egalitarian with age, implicit racial bias appears to remain stable across the lifespan (Baron and Banaji 2006). There are many possible reasons for this, such as social desirability motives increasing as we age.

However, more research is needed to understand this phenomenon. What studies such as Baron and Banaji (2006) indicate, is that there are important age and developmental differences that need to be accounted for in prejudice research.

During these early and crucial formative years, many factors may contribute to the development of racial bias in children. While it has been previously thought that children's strongest racial and ethnic socialisation influencers are within the home and family environment, there has been some contention within the field regarding the strength and complexity of this relationship. Given that school contexts have the potential to guide student attitudes pertaining to race and inclusion it seems logical to explore this space as a possible contributing factor to racial bias in children.

There is a link between children's attitudes regarding race and the attitudes of their teachers. However, additional research is necessary to understand how children develop racially biased beliefs. This will also assist in developing interventions to address racial bias prior to its solidification in adulthood.

Racism, Education and Academic Outcomes

Schools have long been considered a microcosm of broader society and therefore, racism and racial bias may also transcend into a classroom setting. Given children begin primary school during a stage of crucial social-cognitive development, particularly in relation to their ethnic-racial socialisation, it is important to consider how schools may influence this development. Besides, the ultimate objective of education is imparting knowledge to students, enhancing their coping skills, helping them in building their character, and, finally, producing skilled and responsible citizens for nation building. Therefore, schools play an important role in achieving the objective of education and in shaping the career of a child.

Schools are the most common spaces where children experience racism and racial bias (Mansouri and Jenkins 2010). According to Mansouri this can occur from many different sources such as systemically, or from peers, teachers, and other staff members. Teachers' implicit racial bias has the potential to create inequitable learning environments that disadvantage racially marginalised students and privilege white students.

For example, minoritized students are more likely to be suspended or expelled for the same infractions as their white peers. They are also perceived as less cognitive and academically able. Due to these perceptions, minoritized students are more likely to be referred to special education programs and less likely to be referred to gifted education programs, compared to their white peers with similar cognitive abilities.

Teachers' implicit bias has been shown to influence their expectations of students based on their race, such as having lower cognitive and academic expectations for minoritized students compared to majorities students. These implicit biases and differing teacher expectations have been shown to impact students' academic achievement, whereby negative expectations may lead to lower achievement for racially marginalised students.

There is also some evidence that teacher's empathy is diminished when a student belongs to a racial out-group, although there is some debate surrounding this topic. Given teaching professions in the western world are largely comprised of white females, this may have detrimental impacts regarding minoritized students' education opportunities.

Moreover, teachers and school leaders may not be the only ones to embody racial bias or to engage in acts of racism in schools. The literature indicates that not only do children experience racism, but they also have the potential to embody both explicit and implicit racial bias. They also have the potential to act in racially prejudiced ways (Baron and Banaji 2006). For some children, this may result in the development of negative stereotypes that go unchecked, which has the potential to negatively impact minoritized groups through prejudicial beliefs and behaviours. This may sound concerning however, children are also capable of engaging in discussions surrounding racial issues. This indicates an opportunity for early intervention prior to these views becoming ingrained.

Besides, the prevalence and impact of racism and racial bias evident in education is concerning. This is particularly true given that school is often the first encounter young people have with an institution and a space where they spend most of their early and crucial formative years. These incidents of discrimination have detrimental impacts on academic outcomes. For example, experiences of racial bias and racism in classrooms may lead to decreases in academic self-concept and academic achievement.

Racial bias in education may also lead to increases in school suspensions and expulsions of racially minoritized students. These exclusionary experiences may decrease a sense of school belonging in students who experience racism. Additionally, racism at school has long-term consequences that follow students after they have left school, including detrimental impacts felt by families, their communities and society generally (e.g., the school-to-prison pipeline).

Previous research examining racial disparities within educational institutions often avoids discussing the root cause, opting instead to focus on issues such as "racial difference", "culturally responsive pedagogy" or "diversity", circumventing any proper analysis of racism, racial bias, or systemic barriers to achievement. Avoiding identifying racism or racial bias as the root cause of racial disparities in the education system only further perpetuates the cycle of racial injustice that ultimately hinders the achievement of minoritized students and advances the interests of white students.

Despite the growing body of research surrounding the extent and development of racial bias and racism in young children (Baron and Banaji 2006) and within school contexts, there is still a paucity of information regarding the trajectory of this within Australian primary school contexts.

Educational Policies in Australia

Australian teachers are required to have knowledge about teaching culturally and linguistically diverse students (Klenowski & Gertz 2009). This competency is embedded in the Australian Professional Standards for Teachers (Australian Institute for Teaching and School Leadership, 2012) and it is an ideal implied in state and national policy instruments such as The Alice Springs (Mparntwe) Education Declaration (Education Council, 2019). Intercultural understanding also features in the Australian Curriculum as a general capability to be developed across the years of compulsory schooling, adding further impetus for exploring teachers' intercultural understandings.

In addition, teachers must involve parents and carers in planning and implementing the educative process (Australian Institute for Teaching and School Leadership, 2012). This recognises that the views of parents and carers are critical to understanding the education of students from diverse backgrounds.

Roberts, Downes and Reid (2022) conducted a study seeking a change in policies so that Australian students learning standards is enhanced by preparing teachers for rural schools. It was realized that very few rural-teaching units had been offered in teacher education courses, and none of these courses explicitly aimed to prepare teachers for rural teaching.

To them teachers must understand students and their contexts according to Professional Standard in Australia (A national regulator with the primary purpose of improving professional standards for Australian consumers) designed for teaching, arguing a teacher's education that is effective not only require a deep grasping of ruralism or and understanding its challenges, but also a thorough understanding of what is required for rural teaching today in terms of pedagogy. They argued when economic and cultural differences intersect with locational and geographic forms of social difference, there is a lack of teacher preparation that contributes to educational disadvantage. Consequently, they seek a change in policies so that Australian students learning standards is enhanced.

Also, Ingvarson, Beavis and Kleinhenz (2007) conducted a study on education policy withing Victoria/Australia to provide policymakers with guidance about accrediting teacher education programs by providing appropriate standards. In their study, teacher education was found to be crucial. There had been some doubt about the effectiveness, or the necessity, of professional preparation programmes in this field.

In addition, Skourdoumbis (2013) conducted an inquiry and research study focused on the question and concern of teacher effectiveness. Australian education policy development in Victoria was deemed valid and worthwhile when it came to research on classroom schoolteacher effectiveness.

Moreover, because of the 1999 state elections in Victoria, Australian Labor was favoured by the electorate which was prepared to temporarily put aside neoliberal economic rationality policies. Some felt that the policies of the preceding Liberal government had severely damaged the sense of community and connectedness in education across the state. The impact of the Education Reform Act of 1988 in England had already led to similar disenchantment with neoliberal tenets on the other side of the globe.

Australian/Victorian Labor embraced European developments that emphasized the importance of collaborative approaches in twenty-first century education policy, not only desirable but necessary; social equity and school improvement would be promoted by these approaches. Innovation in educational services would also be fostered by them.

Effective teacher accountability systems are essential given the strong link between teacher quality and student learning outcomes. Although all Australian states have implemented policies and practices to increase teacher accountability, it remains doubtful whether they will be able to improve teachers' practice or ensure teacher quality. Besides, in Skourdoumbis's (2014) view, education reform is a representational problem that is "inherently, inevitably political" and current Victorian policy reform targets ineffective and unsuccessful practices, such as classroom instruction and preservice preparation and education.

In the Blueprint for Education, the Victorian State Labour Government outlines its education policies. The Australian Blueprint for Career Development (the Blueprint) is a framework for designing, implementing, and evaluating intentional career development learning for individuals at all ages and stages. A Blueprint identifies a person's knowledge, skills, and attitudes that are essential for making smart career choices and managing their careers effectively.

Career management competencies are referred to in the Blueprint. Blueprint's emphasis on understanding one's preferences and making informed decisions is based on solid career development theory. Professionals with postgraduate qualifications in career development and subject-matter specialists will be the primary users of the Blueprint (G Thompson, 2019).

Educational practice in Australia

While there are policies in place to support inclusion and belonging in schools, the extent to which these policies have been adopted and implemented is less clear. When focusing on racial issues, some educators may shy away from discussions surrounding racism and racial bias due to a lack of knowledge, a lack of confidence, and/or potential biases.

Teaching environments have instead largely advocated for egalitarian and colour-blind approaches to discussing race, which has been shown to have a counterproductive impact that may lead to greater implicit and explicit racial bias, compared to anti-racist curricula. Given that these pedagogical practices appear to disadvantage some students and do not instil an adequate level of cultural or racial competency, there may be a misalignment between policy and practice within some classrooms.

Furthermore, the overwhelming whiteness of the teaching profession, evident in the lack of teachers and leaders from racially diverse backgrounds, may be a contributing factor to the maintenance of inequitable systems. Given the increasing diversity of classrooms, it is imperative that we develop ways to ensure that this diversity is reflected in teaching staff and school leaders. This will assist in providing educational equity for all students, regardless of their race or ethnicity.

1

Motivation, Approaches to Learning, and Retelling

Learning is a long and complex undertaking. The whole person is affected as h/she struggles to reach their potential. Total commitment, total involvement, a total physical, intellectual, and emotional response are necessary to successfully achieve success this chapter will unbundle the term motivation to show its importance in helping students achieve their potential in their learning as well as it will go further to talk about the approaches students take while learning and the theories of learning will be also disclosed. Retelling will be discussed as a pedagogical strategy to enhance Indigenous learners.

Motivation to Learning

Schooling and teaching are social endeavours. In his sociocultural theory of development, Vygotsky emphasized the importance of social contexts in learning and development.

As a social Endeavor, learning involves people of a society co-creating knowledge in distinct cultural and historical contexts (John-Steiner and Mahn, 2003). The sociocultural theory of learning can provide a way to view learning as a continuous dialectic, one that is constantly shifting, making the need for self-regulation and individual innovation even more crucial. In examining the diverse factors that foster and sustain teacher innovation, both perspectives emphasize the social, interactive, and emerging nature of professional the Aboriginal students who have lower levels of than that of the non-Aboriginal students, so that they can improve their socioeconomic and health outcomes by improving their rate of attainment and participation in the education system.

Indigeneity, remoteness, and a non-English speaking background are not the only reasons for high Indigenous failure rates. "Non-performing schools are the principal cause of Indigenous student failure" (Hughes & Hughes, 2012, p.2). From a sociocultural perspective differential performance of Indigenous students may be attributable to real differences in performance because of Indigenous students' differing access to learning, different social, cultural contexts, or real differences in their attainment in the topic under consideration due to their experiences or sociocultural background. And if the curriculum and the school do not contribute to help Aboriginal students understand like the non-Aboriginal so they might be impeding their education and thus the whole country would be affected by such performance. Aboriginal students require ensuring equity in participation, access, and engagement with learning to help learners attain adequate level of academic achievement to empower them in their daily lives.

Measuring Aboriginal students' performance, participation, and educational outcomes allows many researchers to introduce the motivational approaches to the Aboriginal schools in Australia to scaffold the Aboriginal students and eliminate the gap between them and the non-Indigenous students. Through motivation teachers can meet the challenges of better efficiencies, increasing accessibility, lower costs, and greater accomp-lishment in achieving development aims through education.

Motivation is a term derived from the Latin verb for "move", which is the power that causes individual does certain act. It is a constant desire to be fulfilled and arouses actions that result satisfaction by accomplishing the tangible goals (Maslow, 1970. p. 24). Maslow (1970, p.19) proposed that "the whole person is motivated and not just a 'part' of him".

According to Maslow, when the person is hungry, he/she is striving all over and behaves in different way as he used to behave at other times; emotionally changed, his perception towards food changed too. Being hungry drives the person to find food and when he eats the whole body is satisfied and emotionally, he has changed, and this is the case in motivation.

When the students are not interested in the subject, they need somebody to motivate them to help them acquire knowledge. The non-interested person needs motivation to acquire the knowledge just like the hungry person who needs food to satisfy his whole body according to Maslow. So, in the classroom the role of the teacher is to search for a subject that will satisfy the student's interest, or in other words, the students love it so that they get motivated and reach their goals and acquire the learning.

When the teacher finds that the subject is boring and does not meet the students' interest he has to change or look for subjects that evoke the students' interest and sustain their motivation. Students who are motivated, usually, exert strength and are determined to their impending assignment, have aims, needs, and targets, have a sense of concern about dissatisfaction from 'failure', makes acknowledgments regarding achievement and/ or 'failure', are stimulated, and create usage of tactics to help in attaining aims (Gardner, 1972). This means that, learners are motivated to act accordingly in terms of their studying in the class and accomplish better.

Further, the good teacher should help students not only to pass an exam but also to sustain that motivation in the process of teaching. Schimdt, Boraie and Kassabgy (1996, p.14) stated that "integrative-instrumental distinction is similar to intrinsic-extrinsic distinction, but not identical. Both instrumental and integrative motivation can be seen as subtypes of extrinsic motivation because both are related to goals and outcome".

Intrinsic motivation, usually, involves the enthusiasm to integrate in an action for that action is pleasant and sustaining to do. While extrinsic motivation are those actions applied to attain some instrumental end. "People seem to engage in the activities for their own sake and not because they lead to an extrinsic reward.... Intrinsically motivated behaviours are aimed at bringing about certain internally rewarding consequences, namely, feelings of competence and self-determination" (Brown, 2007. p. 172).

Intrinsic motivation is created upon 'innate' desires for proficiency and 'self- determination'. When people are free to choose an activity, they seek interesting situation where they can meet the challenges. To solve these problems, students develop a sense of competence in their abilities.

In contrast to intrinsically motivated behaviours, extrinsic motivation is a concept that relates when an action is done for the purpose of attaining certain separate result. It is usually powered by the expectation of an external prise or avoiding a punishment.

Motivation is significant way of learning that can help in making children creative as well. According to Gallas (2001, p. 460) creativity is "action in the mind and the world", or a more transformation of ideas and images formed by the imagination. Creativity is a process of obtaining original ideas of value. Creativity is also considered as a skill such as, 'creative problem solving' or 'creative thinking' in any learning process which "involves understanding and new awareness, which allows the learner to go beyond notional acquisition, and focuses on thinking skills" (Cachia, R., Ferrari, A., Mutka, K., Punie, Y 2010, p.19).

As Dornyei (2001, p. 116) states, "teacher skills in motivating learners should be seen as central to teaching effectiveness". Perhaps, students are oriented first towards learning by the attitude of their parents or peers towards learning and they are fully interesting to fulfil that study for intrinsic or extrinsic reasons. But in the classroom the students may be influenced with the attitude of the teacher towards the subject. If the attitude of the teacher is positive the student will benefit and be motivated to study. But if the attitude of the teacher is negative, this will lead to demotivation among students.

For example, if the teacher maintains a positive attitude daily in the classroom, this attitude will be reflected on the students, and they become more excited about learning English as well. Therefore, motivation could be highly affected by the attitude of the teacher in the classroom and the relation between attitude and motivation is that both help to support the students' orientation.

On the other side, teachers should be careful in the class that not all students have the same attitude. Negative attitude could be more improved in a class with culturally diverse students. Since different values and culture can make different attitudes as well. Teachers can help in clarifying and giving a new and clear information about what are often legends about other 'cultures' and substitute those legends with correct thoughtful of the other 'culture' as one that differs from individual's culture, so that it could be appreciated and loved (Brown 2007, p. 193). Besides, manner is a good indicator of attitude of the teacher in the classroom.

Teacher must show interest in teaching and treat their students in good and respectful way. The way the teacher talks, the way he/she behaves and the way he/she thinks about the course, his/her knowledge about the course gives positive or negative attitude to the students and they may get motivated or demotivated. Teachers also can motivate students by creating a zero-anxiety learning environment. This gives them the opportunity to express their opinion and encourages them to involve in the teaching process learning one. Also, teacher can ask students to choose the topics they are interested in and encourage them create tasks themselves.

In summary, appropriate teacher's behaviours to motivate students can be addressed throughout four steps:

1) "Enthusiasm
» Share their own positive experiences with students.
» Reminding the students value of the L2 learning as a meaningful experience to achieve their goals in real-life.

2) commitment to and expectations for the students' learning,
» Show the students that they care about students' progress.
» Indicate their physical and mental availability for all things academic.
» Have sufficiently high expectations for what students can achieve.

3) relationship with the students,
» Show students that they accept and care about students.
» Indicate their physical and mental availability.
» Pay attention and listen to each of them.

4) relationship with the students' parents
» Keep parents regularly informed about their children's progress.
» Ask for their assistance in performing supportive task at home." (Dornyei, 2001, p. 32-48).

Therefore, although motivation can play an important role in the knowledge society still there is three main factors that impede improvement in learning: different social, cultural contexts, different access to learning (inequity), and insufficient pedagogy.

Approaches to Learning

Learning is a social process that takes place among all students from different sociocultural and socioeconomic status. Through that process the students are meant to acquire knowledge or skills by being taught by a teacher or experiencing or studying by themselves to get to realize their full potential and determine their future. This process requires each student to follow certain approach that suits his/her intellect abilities and personality.

Three common approaches to learn are there for students to follow to attain their goal; surface approach, deep approach, and achieving approach based on several conceptions of learning (Marton, Dall'Alba, & Beaty, 1993). Some students follow a surface approach through learning to succeed and be promoted to higher level, but others follow a deep approach to comprehend deeply because they are intrinsically interested in learning, and usually they are successful. And other students are motivated to study and love the competition, so they follow the achieving approach to compete with other students. Each student has his/her own way of approaching learning (Bennett, 1999). The interesting thing is why they choose the approach they do....

Some students in a classroom depend on listening to learn, but others depend on watching the teacher to understand. Some would like to work by themselves, others in group. Some can concentrate only in a very calm atmosphere, but others can study even in a very noisy class. In learning English for example among diverse of students with different accents and from different sociocultural and economic status students prefer to study according to their background-using cultural or natural methods comparing to other students.

The process of learning to some students may be impeded due to their cultural background especially for those students who come from remote areas like the Aboriginal students with nonsufficient cultural capital like the non-Aboriginal or refugees who have experienced traumas or migrants. Those students are at risk to fail because of their backgrounds. Understanding the children's preferred learning styles and knowing their educational backgrounds may give the teacher better understanding of choosing the instructional materials.

Acquiring the knowledge or skill requires the student to adapt certain approach which is adequate to their personality, intellect capacity and behaviour (also worth considering their Zone of Proximal Development [Vygotsky] and the social support around them – which could be argued is the most important factor). Some students use surface approach, and others follow deep or achieving approach.

Surface approach is when the students concentrate on reproducing information to fulfil the assessment demands, but it leads to negative feelings about learning. According to (Ramsden, 1992), memorising can be either achieving or deeper approach, depending on the intention of the student. While the surface approach usually leads to vulnerable understarding and achieving and poor approaches to a high leve of understanding, this do not have to be extended to the view that the deeper approach is necessarily adopted by the highly competent students and the surface approach by the weaker ones. While deep approach is obvious when the students concentrate-due to their intrinsic awareness of the material- upon the underlying meaning of the lesson (Kember and Gow 1994).

Adopting an achieving approach is to compete and enhance the self-esteem by attaining the highest grades through assessment. Achieving surface approach and deep approach are together a path to guide the students to reach better understanding and high grades and different rewards (Marton, Hounsell, & Entwistel, 1997). Moreover, there are several theories that can be applied to educational context in educational program that help in creating interest for all learners at different levels. Such as Cognitive Learning, Constructivist Learning, Humanistic Learning, Behavioural Learning, and Postmodern Learning Theories.

In Cognitive Learning Theory, according to Gestalt psychologists the perception of learning must be approached as a pattern rather than the quantity of the component part. Learning is acquired through assimilation (Ausubel, 1963).

Another model of learning was proposed by Bruner (1967) which is the way of thinking. It is gaining a new insight by reconstructing the already known information in a certain way that the learner can see beyond the obvious. Bruner's conceptions of students are that they are information processors, and thinkers (Bigge, 1976). Problem-Based Leaning (PBL) gives one of the best methods to facilitate learner's discovery learning because it gives them the guided practice in the cognitive conflict and inquiry through which learners expand their conceptual framework.

Constructivist Learning Theory is when learning is being viewed by the constructivism as a process of building new knowledge from learner's own experience (Bigge, 1976). A student actively builds or constructs new knowledge based upon current or past knowledge. Constructivism occurs somewhere between humanistic and cognitive views (Kolb, 1984). In that model the role of the instructor is facilitating or encouraging the learners in constructing different knowledge by solving problems. The knowledge building process according to constructivism is viewed both as social and cognitive process.

In Humanistic Learning Theory, Rogers (1969) and Maslow (1970) are the main theorists of this school of thought. According to the above-mentioned theory the instinct encourages students to express themselves and consequently it leads to instinctive behaviour which is inherited and not acquired through experience and occur through stimuli. Students' behaviours result in learners' expression to satisfy their needs.

Behavioural Learning Theory is a learning theory that has the implication that learning is to acquire a new behaviour. Two types of conditioning have been identified by behaviourists as a learning process; classic or operant conditioning-behavioural- that leads to a different behavioural pattern (Quinn, 1995). According to (Burns, 1995) learning is a permanent change in behaviour including observable activities and internal processes such as attitude, emotions and thinking. Based on Post-modern Learning Theory, logic and rationality are not important in acquiring knowledge, and knowledge may be contradictory. The contextual nature of knowledge helps the individual to hold two entirely incongruent view of certain subject at the same time.

In all above theories learning is described as a process and as a product. It is a process of gathering information, store information and apply the information when needed (Ramsden, 1992), and a product of something brought from the outside that results in conditioned learning (Skinner, 1989) or something induced from the inside of a learner which results in insightful learning (Maslow, 1970). The method through which information is processed is based on the characteristic form of thoughts, behaviour, and feelings of the individual and this characteristic form of thoughts, behaviour and feelings makes a student unique and is known as the personality of a person (Jung, 1967). However, just one theory can't explain the process of learning (Quinn, 1995).

Cognitive learning is about how students understand things in terms of their learning style while social learning identifies how meanings and understandings grow out of social encounters. According to Anderson (1983) cognitive learning takes place through dynamic and active mental process. Students select information from the situation, organize that information, link it to what they know, recall what they think to be important, practice the information in adequate contexts, and finally reflect on the attainment of their learning efforts. Learners retain almost two types of information in memory: procedural knowledge and declarative knowledge.

Procedural knowledge is what the learners know "how" to do, for example, reading strategies and problem-solving procedures. And declarative knowledge is "what" the individuals know, such as conceptual and information in science and history. Cognitive theory is also shown to provide explanatory concepts for acquiring a language, language production and comprehension.

Vygotsky's theories about the interaction in cultural contexts to help construction of knowledge are approved by many as a beneficial frame for understanding children's cultural and artistic learning. The theory of the "zone of proximal development" is considered significant in cultural and arts learning, as it is the "region in which the transfer of ability from the shared environment to the individual takes; this means that the distance between the real level of performance the learner can reach unguided and the level of participation probable with the aid of a mentor" (Vygotsky 1978, p. 86, as cited in Robinson.G, Eickelkapm. U, Goodnow.J, Katz. I, 2008, p. 153).

Language and cognition usually interact through how the concepts are kept in memory in procedural and declarative knowledge. According to social constructivism, every child develops in the context of a culture and his learning development is affected by his culture and family environment (Vygotsky, 1934). From Vygotsky's perspective learning, the development of language, articulation of ideas and culture are central to learning and development (Vygotsky, 1934).

Further, several research have revealed that students from cultural diversity tend to exhibit greater diversity in their approaches to learning than students from same cultures (Bennett, 1999). Cognitive constructive learning model would be useful, when teachers teach students from different cultural, social, and linguistic backgrounds such as aboriginal students to find how different culture influence their approaches to learning.

In general, most teachers prefer their students to take a deep and achieving approaches. Deep and achieving approaches strongly influence the quality of students learning outcomes and lead them to high retention and an ability to apply information in new contexts. When students have an opportunity to apply their knowledge, their understanding naturally becomes much more real.

The positive news for teachers is that there are things they can do to influence the approaches that students take - to discourage surface approaches and encourage deep approaches. This is because students' approaches are not fixed characteristics. People often believe that an approach is a characteristic of a student and there are 'deep' students and 'surface' students. But student learning research shows that students' approaches can vary according to students' perceptions of their learning environment.

A student who takes a deep approach to one subject, or even part of a subject, may take a surface approach in relation to something else. We can influence students' approaches by the way we design subjects and courses, particularly the assessment. Inquiring into the approaches that your students are taking and the reasons they give for taking these approaches can be very enlightening, and an excellent way of informing changes to teaching and subjects.

Retelling Story as an Imaginative Approach to Enhance Indigenous Australian Children

The term 'education' involves the recognition of empowering people's social and economic status and differentiating them from non-educated people. It is a significant means by which individuals get to realize their full potential and determine their future. Education is a significant factor that has the potential to empower all students and in particular the Aboriginal students who have lower levels of than that of the non-Aboriginal students, so that they can improve their socioeconomic and health outcomes via improving their rate of attainment and participation in the education system.

Indigeneity, remoteness, and a non-English speaking background are not the only reasons for high Indigenous failure rates. "Non-performing schools are the principal cause of Indigenous student failure" (Hughes & Hughes, 2012, p.2). From a sociocultural perspective differential performance of Indigenous students may be attributable to real differences in performance because of Indigenous students' differing access to learning, different social, cultural contexts, or real differences in their attainment in the topic under consideration due to their experiences or sociocultural background. And if the curriculum and the school do not contribute to help Aboriginal students understand like the non-Aboriginal so they might be impeding their education and thus the whole country would be affected by such performance. Aboriginal students require ensuring equity in participation, access, and engagement with learning to help learners attain adequate level of academic achievement to empower them in their daily lives.

Measuring Aboriginal students' performance, participation, and educational outcomes allows many researchers to introduce the innovative, imaginative, and creative approaches to the Aboriginal schools in Australia to scaffold the Aboriginal students and eliminate the gap between them and the non-Indigenous students.

Through innovation teachers can meet the challenges of better efficiencies, increasing accessibility, lower costs, and greater accomplishment in achieving development aims through education.

> *"Innovation" may be defined as the process of having original thoughts and insights that have value, and then taking initiative to implement the new ideas in ways that touch many people's lives" (Miller, 2009, p.1).*

When teachers are serious in applying innovation while educating students they break down their own out-of-date believes about learning and switch to new images of how they should teach young children and what kind of skills and knowledge they should be aiming for, and designing a classroom environment rich in literacy and in opportunities for its improvement to offer an abundance of materials for oral language activities, reading, and writing (Morrow 1996).

An imaginative approach is a strategy for education innovation that helps make learning meaningful and real. Imagination is the ability of the mind to "combine perceptions from reality into new forms through processes of disassociation and association, developed through the emotions" (Vygotsky 1967/2004 cited in Roppola, T., & Whitington, V 2014, p. 68). According to Alphen (2011, p.2) "Imagination is the ability to picture something in the mind that bears a relationship to a phenomenon from the physical world or other human experience such as the psychological, mythical, spiritual or philosophical". Children between the ages of about 5 to 14 years learn best through the imagination. When teachers appeal to the imagination in their lessons, learners become engrossed in the subject matter and willingly participate in a learning process (Alphen 2011).

Imagination is significant way of innovation that can help in making children creative as well. According to Gallas (2001, p. 460) creativity is "action in the mind and the world", or a more transformation of ideas and images formed by the imagination. Robinson (2006), states that creativity is a process of obtaining original ideas of value. Creativity is also considered as a skill such as, 'creative problem solving' or 'creative thinking' in any learning process which "involves understanding and new awareness, which allows the learner to go beyond notional acquisition, and focuses on thinking skills" (Cachia, R., Ferrari, A., Mutka, K., Punie, Y 2010, p.19).

According to Bidwell and Friedkin (1988) children from higher socioeconomic status (SES) backgrounds performed better than lower SES children across SES measures. Moreover, children exposed to elite culture at home are advantaged in schools (Tzanakis 2011). Bourdieu (1970, 1977) believes that success in the education system is facilitated by the possession of cultural capital and of higher-class habitus. Lower-class pupils do not in general possess these traits, so the failure of most of these pupils is inevitable. For Bourdieu, capital is a source, form of wealth, which produces power. 'Capital is a form of power'. Building from Bourdieu's (1977) notion of cultural capital, parental cultural capital affected children's early and later educational attainment (DiMaggio, 1982).

The term equity derives from a concept of social justice, and it involves the recognition that there are certain things which people should have. Although there are human rights imperative to have equitable opportunity for all people to improve their abilities and participate fully in society, still many outstanding writers, teachers, or scientists are lost because a great number of people cannot obtain the needed learning. According to Bourdieu, the education systems of industrialised societies function in such a way as to legitimate class inequalities.

Equity is important in education but because there is not fairly distribution of opportunity so the talent of some students will be underutilized; some pupils will not develop their abilities and skills with consequent loss to them and to the society generally. "A commitment to equity suggests that differences in outcomes should not be attributable to differences in areas such as wealth, income, power or possessions" (Levin, 2003, P. 5). Equity outcomes of schooling can be measured by linking performance with some factors such as Indigenous status, English language background, disability gender, location, and socioeconomic status. Children in remote areas usually face barriers to accessing educational resources and have fewer of the support services and resources that are available elsewhere. This, of course, widens the gaps between the achievement of Indigenous and other students (Commonwealth of Australia, 2007).

Because Indigenous, refugees and migrant students are more likely to face cultural and linguistic challenges, and their parents might not be able of offering support with their schooling expenses compared with English-speaking parents, the pedagogical strategy: imaginative and critical thinking can contribute to boost indigenous students' performance to maintain social justice and help to improve the economy of the society they are living in as well.

Ryan & Hornbeck (2007), defined pedagogy as the 'art and science of teaching'. They believe that pedagogy is not to be confused with curriculum and involves the cultural, psychological, socio-emotional, and political processes of teaching children. Effective pedagogy incorporates an array of teaching strategies that supports intellectual engagement. Because there is no single, general approach for all situations, teachers must use a group of teaching strategies in different combinations with different groups of students to improve learning outcomes.

Some strategies are suitable for teaching certain fields of knowledge and skill, and some are suitable for certain children backgrounds, abilities, and learning styles. Educational actors with their pedagogical ways have the power to unlock the creative and innovative potential of the young, and to empower them to adapt with the industrialised world, and this, of course, contributes to economic prosperity and to social and individual wellbeing. So, pedagogy can improve teachers' and students' confidence and contributes to build community confidence in the quality of teaching and learning in the school.

Story retelling is an effective pedagogical strategy that can be woven into instruction to increase students' competencies in all areas. Retelling means recounting the story in the child's own words that encourages children to use their imagination, expand their ideas, and create visual images as they transfer the plot [of the story] to new settings, including different characters or new voices.

Moreover, in story retellings, readers or listeners tell what they remember about the story orally or through dramatization, drawing, or writing (Owocki, 1999). Retellings require students to think more conceptually—to look at the bigger picture—rather than answering specific questions about the text. Retelling also helps children internalize information and concepts, such as vocabulary and story structure (Brown & Cambourne, 1987). The more experience children with retelling, are more able to understand, synthesize, and infer because "Retelling is grounded in an understanding of the crucial role that oral language plays in both the formation and sharing of meaning" (Gambrell, Koskinen, & Kapinus, 1991, cited in Gibson, A. Gold, J.& Sgouros, C 2003, p.2).

Engaging children in retelling stories recited to them by teachers or parents is a strategy that is often used to contribute to expressive vocabulary and story-related comprehension (Gambrell & Dromsky, 2000; Geva & Olson, 1983; Soundy, 1993). Learning experiences that happen before, after and during reading has great influence on students' literacy development. After reading a story the children try to retell the story in their own words. This technique ties into these learning experiences and is an effective way to boost children's reading comprehension. Story retelling requires young children to focus on the larger picture of the story rather than answer specific question about the details of the story and therefore lets the educator to see how well a student understands the story.

> *"Retelling has been found to significantly improve story comprehension, sense of story structure, and oral language complexity"* (Koskinen et al, 1988, p. 892).

As a comprehension strategy, retelling stories encourages students to pay attention to the meaning of the text, strengthens elements of story structure, for example, setting character, and plot, requires readers to differentiate between supporting details and key ideas, and finally encourages communication as well as oral language development. As an assessment strategy, it demonstrates what the student comprehends and remembers about the story, reveals what the learner considers essential about the story, indicates what learners know about literary language and story structure, and demonstrates the learners' oral language development and vocabulary.

Moreover, when students are asked to retell a story, they might be working individually or in pairs to write their retell. Children will be taught to use a sequence of questions that encourages retelling. In the first stages of instruction, it is vital to limit the amount of writing used so that the focus of the instruction is on the skill. It can begin by using single sentences.

When students become skilled the amount of text could be gradually increased from sentences to paragraphs, to more paragraphs, to chapters, and to end with books. Before reading, teacher will teach unfamiliar vocabulary so that all children understand the plot of the story. By having young children retell the story in their own words, teachers can identify student's strength, and particular areas of difficulty that encounter individual students (Gibson, A. Gold, J. & Sgouros, C 2003). Also, the teacher can help the child while retelling a story by asking open-ended questions if the child pauses or get confused. The goal of this should encourage children to think critically about the plot and to improve their vocabulary and comprehension. As young children are motivated to retell stories, their listening skills and language will improve.

Most young students can develop literacy and numeracy skills throughout retelling stories. However, for Indigenous students still it is more problematic. Indigenous students like to read only if they have to or to get the information they need. The reason can be related to their attitude towards how to learn based on their own culture, parental importance, and traditional habits.

Indigenous languages were not written lan-guages, and information was conveyed in stories, songs, dances, and painting.

Therefore, the teacher can apply interesting subjects to Aboriginal students for encouraging them to read more. Introducing students to a range of dreaming stories is one approach that teacher can follow to bridge knowledge to them. Vygotsky's theories about the interaction in cultural contexts to help construction of knowledge are approved by many as a beneficial frame for understanding children's cultural and artistic learning. The theory of the "zone of proximal development" is considered significant in cultural and arts learning.

Dreaming stories are stories that belong to Indigenous Australians' for teaching a lesson or explaining the creation of something. Australia has two indigenous peoples or original inhabitants- the Torres Strait Islander and the Aboriginal peoples- who have been living in Australia with their religious or spiritual beliefs for possible up to 60 000 years and are the conservators of one of the world's ancient continuing cultural.

In addition to the traditional Indigenous languages, creoles, the language that derives from language contact are spoken by Indigenous inhabitants of northern Australia. Every Australian Indigenous' language is related to an area of land and has a deep spiritual importance. In distant age these different languages came to ancestral people of Indigenous Australians that some call 'the Dreamtime'. 'Traditional Australian Indigenous stories are often referred to as Aboriginal Dreaming stories or Torres Strait Islander legends and sometimes as creation stories' (Aboriginal education for all learners in South Australia, p. 20). Considering dreaming stories not only can be useful for Indigenous students, but also it is good for improving non-Indigenous students' knowledge about Aboriginals' culture and prepare teachers to work productively with Indigenous students.

Regarding the qualification of non-Indigenous teachers there is a major body of literature proves that non-Indigenous teachers in Australia do not have enough knowledge about knowledge and identities, suitable pedagogies for the ways of teaching indigenous children, and the complexities of indigenous cultures (Brayboy & Maughan, 2009; Partington, 2003; Villegas, Neugebauer, & Venegas, 2008).

Aboriginal students are coming from a diverse range of lands. These students' first language is other than English. Their life experience is often significantly different from that which they encounter in the classroom among non-Indigenous students. When teachers and students come from different cultural backgrounds, conflicts are more likely to happen and it can exacerbate the difficulties that teachers may have with classroom management (Weinstein, Tomlinson-Clarke & Curran, 2004). These raise challenges for teachers who are faced with classes made up of a combination of Aboriginal and non-Aboriginal students.

Teachers would like to manage diversity by making sure that all students feel comfortable in their classroom. However, they are not exactly confident how to achieve this task. Sometimes they want to incorporate the cultural heritages of students in curriculum, but that culture might be considered wrong in their own cultural traditions. They want to use appropriate discipline practices but do not always understand the behaviour of their students. Many educators, struggle to really know Aboriginal students. One main reason for this is that "Aboriginal people have their own ways of looking at and relating to the world, and the universe, and each other" (Barnhardt & Kawagley, 2005, p.10, cited in Santoro, N., Reid, J., Crawford, L 2011, p.68). Therefore:

> *"Teachers need to distinguish the "funds of knowledge" that Indigenous students draw on and how teachers need to adopt culturally responsive pedagogy to open up the curriculum and assessment practice to allow for different ways of knowing and being" (Klenowski & Gertz 2009, p. 36).*

Understanding the history and perspective of Aboriginal peoples is important for non-Indigenous students as well. To better integration between Aboriginal and non-

Aboriginal students' events of cultural-historical, and religious that affect concepts of Aboriginal identity within Australia must be explored by mainstream of society.

In their planning, teachers can consider cultures related to Aboriginal and Torres Strait Islander peoples as well as non-Aboriginal people and give students opportunities to retell a variety of story from different Australian cultures including those of Aboriginal and Torres Strait Islander peoples and non-Aboriginal for expression of their cultural identity.

Cultural identity involves all beliefs, the way we see the universe and ourselves, and the way we communicate. To develop conveying educational services to Aboriginal children it is essential to involve them at grass roots, and understanding strategies that will lead them to improvements. "Cultural learning and comprehension occur in a process of interaction between children and adults, in which adults guide children's behaviour as an essential element in concept acquisition/acculturation/education" (Cole 1985, p. 158, as cited in Robinson. G, Eickelkapm. U, Goodnow. J, Katz. I 2008, p. 153).

In addition, nowadays it is generally agreed that the maintenance of a children's first language is essential to their success in acquiring a second language. In context of Australian schools, most of Aboriginal children speak Aboriginal English (AE), a diversity of English that varies from the Standard Australian English (SAE) requisite in schools. According to Butcher (2008, p. 625), "Many of the 455,000 strong Aboriginal population of Australia speak some form of Australian Aboriginal English (AAE) at least some of the time and it is the first (and only) language of many Aboriginal children. This means their language is somewhere on a continuum ranging from something very close to Standard Australian English (SAE) at one end, through to something very close to [a] creole at the other".

Moreover Zubrick et al. (2006) approve that the academic performance of learners who speak Aboriginal English (AE) are three times lower than the other students. Therefore, besides of other learning practices, engaging Aboriginal students in retelling story by the teacher can be a useful strategy to enhance their learning process in acquiring the second language. As previously mentioned, the procedure of retelling story tends to highlight the importance of several practices including reading a story to students, actively engaging them in reading those stories, rereading the story to them, can develop their deep involvement in the stories, by asking the student to retell the story, and develop their verbal elaborations and comprehension (Isbel, 2002).

Furthermore, the first language plays significant role in acquiring a second language and can introduce the students to the new culture of new worlds. 'It is an obvious yet not generally recognized truism that learning in a language which is not one's own provides a double set of challenges, not only is there the challenge of learning a new language but also that of learning new knowledge contained in that language' (UNESCO, 2003).

In conclusion, Aboriginal perspectives are based on Aboriginal cultures that express itself in a different way with different stories, art, cultural products, dance, and music. To integrate them into existing pedagogy, greater attention of Indigenous culture, and understanding of their identity is necessary. When teachers are faced with Aboriginal students or refugee/migrants, they have high responsibilities towards in teaching and they need to exert more effort to understand how promote students' involvement in learning.

Pedagogies that engage students' imagination and creativity offer teachers the opportunity to achieve this goal. Many teachers value imagination and creativity but may do not know how to foster this ability in the classroom to meet the needs of Aboriginal students. Hence, retelling Dream stories is a useful way to improve literacy learned process and acceptance of Aboriginal students' home background language, culture, and identity.

Story telling is an integral part for Aboriginal people as well as for all students that place a main role in education children from the early age. Adults take responsibility for passing on the stories to the next generations. The stories of the Dreaming reveal the history story and cultural of Indigenous people. The stories are an education tools in guiding children on how to behave with the universe and each other. Retelling Dream story can help teachers as facilitators of the passing on of traditional culture and knowledge to young Aboriginal children as well as refugees/migrants in formal education setting.

Therefore, Aboriginal students can develop the positive self- identity through learning their own cultures, histories, values, and lifestyles. Participating in learning also will equip them with skills and knowledge needed to integrate in the mainstream society as well as cultural realities of their communities.

2

Multicultural Education in Australia and Victoria

The Australian context is becoming diverse. The development of multicultural education has been introduced to help diverse students achieve equity in education. This chapter will define the term multicultural and the Implementation of Multicultural Education because of bias and racism; a problem that affects people all over the world will be discussed in detail. As well as the preparing of preservice teacher to Australian/Victorian students with extensive support needs will be explored.

Australian Context

There is an increasing number of multicultural classrooms in Australia. Many students are coming from a diverse range of countries. For many of these students, their first language is other than English. Their life experience is often significantly different from that which they encounter in Australia.

In the past decade, 4000 refugees have settled in Victoria, Australia, where the study is based. Children and young adults make up a large portion of these refugee. According to the Department of Education, 13,000 students from refugee and asylum-seeking backgrounds attended Victorian government schools in 2018 (Department of Education 2021). Refugee children often experience a range of difficulties witness or experience violence and death.

However, as large numbers of immigrant or refugee children enter mainstream schools on global scale, schools and teachers are challenged to develop programs and teaching methods that meet the specific language needs of these children. Globalization is inconceivable in today's world. Multinational corporations and foreign learning opportunities are defining current economic development. Due to all of these changes, it has become crucial to develop skills that facilitate communication among people with different backgrounds, habits, and attitudes, which will enhance intercultural understanding (Vegh and Nguyen Luu, 2019).

Multicultural Education

The development of multicultural education according to Sleeter (1994) like in the United Kingdom, Australia and Canada has its roots in slavery, immigration, colonisation, and the subjection of the Indigenous population.

Multiculturalism is a concept which was perceived by difference in ethnic or race background. Some multicultural constructs which involve several characteristics emerged from the interaction of experienced sociological, geographical, and economic elements linked to developments accumulated by the course of history. Thoughts regarding the concept of multiculturalism that includes recognition of elements such as, ethnic background, race, age sexual preference, disability, language, religious and social class denomination have been defined better because of its inclusion in the education system.

Multicultural education is a complete school reform process that seeks to provide a fundamental standard of education for every student where segregation and racism is rejected, and diversity of society students is supported. Multicultural education has been described as a type of education where students from different races, genders, ethnic and cultural backgrounds are to be given the same opportunity of success in their learnings. This type of education was aimed to guarantee equality of opportunity, to resolve problems arising from cultural disputes, and to help students to develop empathy to recognize their common cultures, and in doing that they increase their academic success.

Multicultural education is significant in providing comprehensive educational system where individuals in multicultural societies can live together in peace. Multicultural education is a form of education that champs freedom: the actions of the theoreticians and researchers of the multicultural teaching movement in trying to reform educational organizations support the declaration that this is an actual reform movement. So, all students from different ethnic and cultural backgrounds can gain knowledge, attitudes and skills that can help in making better future of their own people and the planet in a productive manner.

Moreover, multicultural teaching is a comprehensive school reform process aiming to provide the fundamental standard of education for every student and one in which the diversity of society members is supported, and segregation and racism is rejected. Besides, multicultural education correlate schooling and education designed for the cultures of many different races in the educational system. And multicultural education aims to support students in acquiring behaviours such as showing respect, establishing empathy with, and acting towards the others tolerantly. It attempts to allow students to provide themselves with the essential knowledge, behaviours, and skills to participate in democratic society. Hence, multicultural education is more crucial than ever in breaking down stereotypes, intolerance, and bullying within schools; ensuring our new citizens feel welcome and included in their newly adoptive society.

The Implementation of Multicultural Education

Despite considerable public support within Australia for cultural diversity (Markus, 2014 Dandy and Pe-Pua, 2010) national and international contexts, especially since 2001, have seen heightened anxieties around immigration and social cohesion. These have exacerbated ongoing concerns regarding the lack of clarity about what multiculturalism means, the ways in which multicultural policy is currently managed and its usefulness within twenty-first century nation states.

Multicultural education and bilingual education had been implemented attempted to solve the problem of language and racial discrimination in education. However, problems related to cultural diversity are still occurring nowadays and are much more complex and problematic than decades ago.

According to the multicultural approach, race, ethnicity, and culture should be paid attention to, group differences should be valued, and individuals should learn about the perspectives of various groups in society. Supporters of the multicultural approach argue that to reduce prejudice, it is not necessary to remove intergroup categories. Instead, it is assumed that learning about and critically reflecting on diversity can reduce prejudice and foster intercultural competence. Schools should not only focus on prejudice reduction, but should also include cultural content in the curriculum, and foster understanding of implicit cultural assumptions and perspectives.

In conceptualizations of classroom cultural diversity climate, multicultural approaches are often subsumed under labels such as "cultural socialization", "promotion of cultural competence". Hence, multicultural education may affect those aspects of multicultural competence.

Through the norms of knowledge that teachers honour, offer, and symbolize, anti-racist education may be able to reflect our culturally diverse, multicultural society. Racism has been a key barrier to education. Generally, marginalized groups don't have to be intentionally discriminated against for negative responses to arise (Baron & Banaji, 2006; Sue et al., 2007, cited in Yared, Grové and Chapman, 2020). A personal explicit racial bias appears to be significantly more equal than tacit racial bias (Baron & Banagi, 2006).

Bias and racism are a problem that affects people all over the world (Baron and Banaji, 2006; Hall et al., 2015; Pager and Shepherd, 2008; Paradies and Cunningham, 2009; Vaught and Castagno, 2008; Sue et al., 2007a,b, cited in Yared, Grové and Chapman, 2020). Racism and racial bias have a pervasive and prevalent impact, making their analysis crucial. Among the impacts of such behaviour are lowered empathy from individuals outside their own group diminished health outcomes as well as anxiety and depression. Most previous studies investigating racism and racism bias have focused on people outside the Australian context. Additionally, it is unclear how racial bias and racism affect educational settings (Yared, Grové and Chapman. 2020).

Multicultural Education in Australia

Education systems in Australia are varied and diverse. Whether in public or private schools, suburbs or remote Aboriginal communities, a common goal is student engagement. The annual cycle of reporting on the educational outcomes of Aboriginal students in literacy and numeracy, along with other key target areas continues to demonstrate the largely unchanged levels of underachievement of these students. This failure has been largely evidenced at both state and commonwealth levels across Australia.

Notwithstanding gains and losses at individual schools, there has been no significant improvement in the overall performance of Aboriginal students in national and State tests—either in terms of absolute performance or in terms of the gap between Aboriginal and non-Aboriginal students.

Multicultural Education in Victoria/Australia

Victoria is home to one of the most culturally diverse societies in the world and is also among the fastest growing and most diverse states in Australia. At the 2016 Census, Victoria's population was 5.93 million. It increased by 10.7% since 2011, compared to 8.8% for the whole of Australia.

Of Victoria's total population:

> » 28.4% were born overseas in over 200 countries.
> » 49.1% were born overseas or born in Australia with at least one parent born overseas.
> » 26% spoke a language other than English at home.
> » 59% followed one of more than 130 different faiths Victorian Government (www.vic.gov.au)

According to Victoria State Government's website, the Department of Education and Training offers learning and development support, services, and resources for all Victorians, from birth through to adulthood (2017). Multicultural education also makes sure that all students have access to inclusive teaching and learning experiences. These experiences will allow students to successfully take part in a rapidly changing world where cross-cultural understanding and intercultural communication skills are essential.

In a school context, and with the support of school policies and programs, multicultural education helps students develop:

- Proficiency in English.
- Competency in a language or languages other than English.
- In depth knowledge and awareness of their own and other cultures.
- An understanding of the multicultural nature of Australia's past and present history.
- An understanding of, and skills to interact in, intercultural settings.
- An appreciation of the importance of local, national, and international interdependence in social, environmental, economic, and political arenas and an understanding that mutual support in these areas is vital to local and global harmony.
- Schools should make sure multicultural perspectives are incorporated into all aspects of school life by:
- Promoting diversity as a positive learning experience.
- Incorporating multicultural perspectives across all learning domains.
- Incorporating multicultural, anti-racism, and human rights perspectives in school policies and practices.

» Enhancing teachers' and students' intercultural understanding and cross-cultural communication skills.

» Making sure all school policies, including three year strategic and annual plans, codes of conduct, dress codes and discipline policies reflect the diverse nature of the school community.

Australian/Victorian Students with Extensive Support Needs

Students with diverse needs are more likely to be supported by teachers who create a social ecology. By understanding students' social roles and relationships within the classroom (i.e., social dynamics), teachers can guide instruction and classroom behaviour management practices (Farmer et al., 2019). The educational experience of many students with extensive support needs (ESN) is enhanced by the provision of specific instruction as well as a variety of communication supports.

Preservice special education teachers are not adequately prepared to implement evidence-based practices and supports addressing the communication needs of students with ESN, despite evidence-based practices and supports being identified (Walker et al., 2022). It is becoming increasingly important for teachers to integrate more intercultural elements into their classrooms. In practice, however, it is often unclear how to do so (Roiha and Sommier, 2021).

Public schools within an Australian context, the State of Victoria are particularly vulnerable to academic underperformance, low-performing and economically and socially disadvantaged schools (Skourdoumbis, 2013). The main findings of Skourdoumbis's (2013) indicates that education policy actors advocate a strong belief in particular forms of evidence-based research for the development of education policy in classroom teacher effectiveness.

Research evidence indicates three key features of our school system that need to be addressed:

> 1) In some schools and some regions, poor outcomes are concentrated. There is a diverse range of student needs in these schools and regions. The school needs to address core learning areas, create a culture of high expectations and address absenteeism and student transition issues.

> 2) In a given school, there are often large differences between classes in terms of outcomes. The relationship between teaching and learning is therefore central. The quality of the teaching, the leadership of the school and the environment (including the relationship with the community) all play a role in this relationship.

> 3) Despite similar student populations, schools' outcomes differ. A culture of continuous school improvement must be built for schools to improve, and this shows that schools can improve (Skourdoumbis, 2013).

Also, according to (Collucci, 2022) regarding multilingual students in a context where social and political contexts don't necessarily recognize the importance of linguistically responsive teaching, there is a pressing need to explain how teachers who are not specifically certified to teach English language learners (ELLs) can become more responsive to linguistic differences in their practices.

The current development of linguistically responsive teaching is influenced both by Freire's (1970; 2000, cited in Collucci, 2022) emphasis on dialogue and respectful education. For individuals to be successful, education must provide them with the tools for learning, thinking, and participating (Collucci, 2022). Educators' practices are not just influenced by their personal knowledge, skill, disposition, and goals; they are also influenced by their colleagues, schools, policies, and national discourses (Romijn, Slot and Leseman, 2021).

3

Cultural Competence

Various attempts at defining cultural competence to provide a clear understanding of the concept is made in this chapter. These various definitions highlight the importance of schools in bringing about effective and meaningful change concerning multicultural classroom management.

Classroom management is affected by the way intercultural competence is applied, but its production is complex. There are no practical plans for managing classrooms with culturally diverse students, despite extensive research on management strategies for multicultural classrooms and cultural competence among teachers. There are challenges of teaching a diverse classroom because of similarities in complications and alteration, one may now handle professionally managing the whole processing, have appropriate responses, providing constitutionally right responses, and covering many sources of that perspective. Being culturally competent entails being aware of cultural social aspects of teaching or learning.

This chapter will define cultural competence and unbundle its four components. Then it will go further to explore the multicultural competence in Australia.

Cultural Competence

> *"Cultural competence is the ability to participate ethically and effectively in personal and professional intercultural settings. It requires being aware of one's own cultural values and world view and their implications for making respectful, reflective, and reasoned choices, including the capacity to imagine and collaborate across cultural boundaries." (Nechifor and Borca, 2020, p. 11).*

Before defining cultural competence, it is necessary to clarify the term "culture". A culture is composed of different layers, such as material culture (e.g., clothes or food), social culture (e.g., social rules), and subjective culture (e.g., values and attitudes). Whether it is a nation, a generation, or a social class, culture is shared by a group of people. The culture of one's collective is usually only adopted to a certain extent, and there are often elements of more than one culture incorporated into the collective culture. In interpreting, judging, and reacting to others' thinking and behaviour, one's cultural influences determine what is perceived as normative (Schwarzenthal et al., 2020).

The concept of cultural competence is defined as attitudes, behaviours, and policies that can work together in situations where cultural differences exist (Shantanam and MUELLER, 2018). Urban school districts in Australia/Victoria are examples of urban, cross-cultural settings. Operationally defined, cultural competence entails the integration and transformation of knowledge about individuals and groups of people into specific standards, policies, practices, and attitudes used in appropriate cultural settings to increase the quality of services, thereby producing better outcomes.

Cultural competence conveys the idea of individuals being able to acquire the knowledge, skills, and dispositions that allow them to effectively work in cross-cultural settings and rests on the belief that individuals can effectively function, communicate, and coexist in settings with individuals who possess cultural knowledge and skills that differ from their own.

With reference to literatures, Cultural Competence was also termed Ethnic Competence and Cultural Awareness, which has been described by different researchers from different point of views. However, many researchers finally converge on the term "Cultural Competence" (Cross, Bazron, Dennis, & Issacs, 1989; Lum, 2005). DuPraw and Axner (1997) focused on how to develop cultural competence and mentioned the following guidelines: Learn from generalizations about other cultures, respect others' choices, don't assume that there is one right way to communicate, listen enthusiastically, respect others' choices, don't pre-judge, be open to learning more about them and have an awareness of current power imbalances. To work with diverse populations in the United States, psychotherapists need cultural competence. This competency consists of knowledge, skills, and attitudes that are difficult to integrate.

One of the significant aspects of creating cultural competence begins with developing a more nuanced understanding of culture and its complexities. Much of the important work that is associated with culture, cultural knowledge. A plethora of research documents how culture influences cognition, motivation, and behaviour. Much of this work has been cantered on the idea that culture is not static across groups, but is constantly changing, deeply complex, highly nuanced, and manifested differently across and within groups.

Cultural competence is the interaction of awareness of one's own cultural worldview, towards cultural differences, knowledge of different cultural practices and worldviews, and cross-cultural skills at a point in time that enables a teacher to understand, communicate with, and effectively interact with students in a multicultural classroom (DTUI, 2011). This information can help decide what activities, exercises, and experiences are necessary to improve student's level of multicultural skills and sensitivity. Multicultural competencies are a significant heuristic tool for helping students develop the necessary knowledge, skills, and awareness to work effectively with culturally different students form themselves.

> *'Cultural competence requires that organizations have a defined set of values and principles, and demonstrate behaviours, attitudes, policies and structures that enable them to work effectively cross culturally.' (National Centre for Cultural Competence, 2006).*

Becoming culturally competent means building respectful relationships. This happens through our communication with others, through our daily experiences in local communities with children and families. Mainly it is about what we do every day, the decisions we make and the words we utter, as it is much about what we believe, what we understand and what we think. Although it is profound, interconnected and sometimes a complex, it is the most important way that we can guarantee that Australia remains such a place of peace and justice for its citizens.

Cultural competence is a term used to describe how individuals and services work effectively to support, embrace, and promote cultural difference. Becoming culturally competent is a strong expectation of the National Quality Framework (NQF) and performs better in the Early Years Learning Framework (EYLF) as well as the National Quality Standard (NQS). It is something for every person to consider while practicing with children and their families regardless of where we are in Australia, or the variety of diversity occurs in the communities we are part of.

Cultural competence includes our efforts to evaluate and build connections with Torres Strait Islander and Aboriginal Peoples. Programs that share and highlight Australia's rich Aboriginal culture with all children contribute to reconciliation and support the rights of all people to be valued. May be the most important reason to consider cultural competence is that, by recognizing more about and respecting our different cultural ways of being, we are creating children's services that welcome everybody, create a sense of belonging for children and equip them all to live well with diversity. Taking practical actions towards cultural competency it is a good idea to start locally with children and families that we know well. As we gain the knowledge more and become more confident, we can develop our competency further.

Cultural competency can start with our local community. Gaining our knowledge and developing positive attitudes towards different cultures can make us aware of what is happening locally and make us understand what is important to the community people. Communities develop and change; people of the community bring with them cultural perspectives and values. And services that respond to neighborhood cultural features and local events make cultural competency a meaningful and relevant experience. Celebrations are the easiest way for us teachers, families, and children- to gain knowledge about each other and become culturally competent. Perhaps the main celebration for all is birthday parties.

Besides, DuPraw and Axner (1997) focused on how to develop cultural competence and mentioned the following guidelines: Learn from generalizations about other cultures, respect others' choices, don't assume that there is one right way to communicate, listen enthusiastically, respect others' choices, don't pre-judge, be open to learning more about them and have an awareness of current power imbalances.

There are four component model of cultural competence as the underpinning framework for the analyzing of teachers' cultural competence (DTUI, 2011). In this model, cultural competence is the interaction of awareness of one's own cultural worldview, attitude towards cultural differences, knowledge of different cultural practices and worldviews, and cross-cultural skills at a point in time that enables a teacher to understand, communicate with, and effectively interact with students in a multicultural classroom.

Further, multicultural awareness "is central to what we see, how we make sense of what we see, and how we express ourselves" (DuPraw & Axner, 1997). Multicultural knowledge includes the accumulation and internalization of specific knowledge regarding diverse groups (Sue et al., 1982). Attitudes towards cultural differences are defined as a hypothetical construct that represents teacher's degree of like or dislike for cultural differences.

Moreover, negative attitude can lead teachers to misinterpretation of behaviours and inequitable treatment of culturally different students (Weinstein, Tomlinson-Clarke, & Curran, 2004). Cross-cultural skills also are a set of behaviors that teachers apply through interactions with culturally diverse students (Sue & Sue, 1990). Previous research shows that teachers feel different degrees of competency in many components of cultural competence (Holcomb-McCoy, 2005; King, 2004). Teachers perceived high levels of cultural awareness but were unsure about their levels of cultural knowledge and skills (Henkin & Steinmetz, 2008; Martines, 2005). Teachers' attitudes also improved as they developed an increased awareness of and appreciation toward other cultures (Cho, DeCastro-Ambrosetti, 2006).

Besides, the National Centre for Cultural Competence (2008) offers a cultural competence framework that consists of five key concepts: (1) valuing diversity; (2) conducting ongoing self-assessment; (3) the ability to manage the dynamics of difference; (4) the willingness to acquire and institutionalize cultural knowledge; and (5) the ability to adapt to diversity and the cultural contexts of the communities that the individual serves. These five concepts provide a comprehensive account of how individuals must remain reflective about their beliefs, behaviours, and dispositions, while also recognizing how the cultural knowledge of others holds as much value for them as others hold for their own (American, 2022).

1-Multicultural Knowledge

Multicultural education means learning of appropriate knowledge, skills, ad attitudes related to the appreciation and respect of diverse cultures and other differences such as race, religion, ethnicity etc. Multicultural knowledge includes the accumulation and internalization of specific knowledge regarding diverse groups (Sue et al., 1982). Multicultural knowledge may be built upon good family connections. Connections that will lead to beneficial communication skills with different culture and understanding of the habits of diverse students.

For the people who have incomplete, inaccurate, or biased knowledge regarding various cultures, this information base should be corrected before multicultural education can proceed. Knowledge relates to familiarity with theories and concepts about prejudice and specific knowledge about different cultures or the skills to learn about them.

2-Attitudes Towards Cultural Differences

Attitude is a concept to understand man behaviour. It is a complex mental state including believes and feelings. Attitudes towards cultural differences are defined as a hypothetical construct that represents teacher's degree of like or dislike for cultural differences. Positive attitudes regarding multicultural education are defined as being tolerant and respectful to diverse cultures to ensure equality of opportunities in education away from discrimination of race, religion, or language.

While negative attitude can lead teachers to misinterpretation of behaviours and inequitable treatment of culturally different students (Weinstein, Tomlinson-Clarke, & Curran, 2004). It was found that a collective understanding which separates people from category or group from others, is a sequence of shared attitudes, beliefs, values, and behaviours passed from one generation to the other. The major aims of multicultural education are expression of values and attitudes, equality and excellence in education, the acquisition of the basic skills, and the promotion of cultural and ethnic education as well as personal development. Teachers influence the interactions among students.

When teachers have positive attitude towards multicultural education, respect for cultural differences, respect all students from different abilities and perspectives, and value diversity, students from diverse cultures learn how to recognize cultural differences and be aware of the diverse cultures around them. Teachers with their reflection of positive or negative attitude while communication with students shape their lives and impact their attitudes towards themselves and the public, affect development of communication, be creative and research.

Besides, teachers are valuable in the success and failure of any program; their role in the primary classrooms is of primary importance to the children from the minute they enter the classroom. Teachers' positive attitudes, values, expectations, and beliefs are critical in creating beneficial and safe classroom climate in which all learners can succeed.

Positive attitudes lead to success, but negative attitudes lead to failure thus as a result success leads to positive ego attitude while failure can lead to negative ego attitudes. Teacher's positive attitude affects the student's attitude towards school- work and school, the student's self-confidence, motivation, and as a result his/her personality development. Teaching is saying and explaining. One of the basic principles of teaching qualifications is to support the student by the teacher and to the teacher to put his/her positive expectations to motivate the students to learn. While the positive attitude allows the teacher to create a positive relation with students, also, it allows the teacher to indulge in the positive behaviour of students as opposing to the negative behaviour, taking on a supporting role as well.

Moreover, teachers who try to understand students' emotions such as fear, worry, and interest, support students; social activities, appreciate, approve of, and compliment them for activities they find of value will make the students understand that they are being thought of, aided, and loved, and that the teachers are working for their good. Students of such teachers will, taking the teachers as role model, in turn be mindful of others, willing to the aid of others, keeping positive attitudes and good relations.

3-Cross-Cultural Skills

Multicultural skills facilitate meaningful and effective interaction such as pursuing consultation necessary with people with different cultural background. Multicultural and global educators approve that if teachers are to develop cross-cultural competence, knowledge, and skills, they need face-to face experiential learning about people different from them. Cross cultural skills are considered a significant contribution to the personal and professional progress of pre-service teachers (PST).

The theory behind dialogic teaching, which is embedded in socio-cultural theory, was represented by Vygotsky (1978). It is based on the belief of a close relationship among speaking, thinking, and learning. It is critical to enable teacher education students to start diverse skills in different socio-cultural contexts and to educate them to comprehend instruction and learning in multicultural setting and developing the student's skills to work with multi-ethnic classes with learners from different cultural backgrounds. Vygotsky and other ideologists defend the significance of the role social skills have in effective learning, while the learners' knowledge about each other might increase their confidence, problem solving and communication among each other in constructive and tolerant way.

4-Multicultural Awareness

Multicultural awareness "is central to what we see, how we make sense of what we see, and how we express ourselves" (DuPraw & Axner, 1997). It consists of the self-awareness, attitudes, values, beliefs, and assumptions crucial to serve culturally different students from oneself.

One of the basic elements of any educational program is certainly the educators themselves. The success of formal teaching is connected to the professional preparedness and attitude of the teachers themselves. This highlights the importance of the qualities of the educators themselves and the multicultural elements lurk in and related to these qualities. Generally, educators perceived beliefs, values, and events in standard conditions, and educated regarding they knew themselves. Because they did not realize the ethnic, racial, social, or linguistic diversities of their learners, they knowingly or unknowingly practiced the wrong teaching techniques in their classes.

To allow the educators to deliver effective teaching in multicultural classes, the educators must be encouraged to engage cultural sensitivity strategies and guarantee equality of opportunity to ensure personal development and academic success of all students.

Multicultural Competence in Australia

Along with effective curriculum and pedagogy, a teacher multicultural competence is an important part of multicultural classroom management. Teachers are the foundational building blocks in the classroom construction and addressing the management of diversity in the classroom starts with them. Their ability to investigate different cultural world views, interpret and adapt them in many ways for the benefit of the students has also proved to be very beneficial (Bennett, 1986).

Education is considered a key factor for success and opportunity. Although there is substantial evidence suggesting that a variety of barriers exist within education that negatively influence students from minority backgrounds, there is substantial evidence suggesting that a variety of barriers exist within education that negatively affect pupils from minority backgrounds (Yared, Grové, & Chapman, 2020). These barriers exist at a personal level (e.g., racial bias and microaggressions from educators and peers). Understanding how those issues are addressed and unfolded is complex and multifaceted.

According to Australian Census 2006, Victoria is a multicultural society comprising people from more than 200 nations, speaking more than 200 languages and dialects, and following more than 120 faiths. Multicultural education is not a mainstream issue in Australia. Australian classrooms are full of children from a range of cultural backgrounds and government's aim is to bring about integration of students from different cultural backgrounds and provide equal educational opportunities for all of them.

However, when I came to Australia as a mother of four children in different grades, I realised that my children usually experience cultural dissonance when their Australian teacher misinterprets their cultural pattern of learning, communication, and behaviour. I also knew that some students fail in their study due to the misunderstanding. This issue is not only restricted to the students but also to the teachers themselves.

Although most of the teachers are qualified, sometimes they fail to control and convey information in a multicultural classroom. Usually, teachers apply classroom management styles which result from their cultural assumptions, and this can be inappropriate for students from backgrounds that are not the same as the teacher. The dominant cultural values that underpin many Australian schools are a result of the cultural backgrounds of many teachers and are from a white, middle-class perspective. Diversity of students' backgrounds in Australian schools demands teachers become more multiculturally competent.

On the other side, Australian schools have received a growing number of students with a refugee-background. Although most teachers have had experience with students from culturally and linguistically diverse backgrounds in their classroom, many will not have worked with students with refugee experience.

Working with students with refugee experience can be challenging specially in primary schools since refugee students are newly arrived in the classroom situation. Many of them have had to flee their homes, have been separated from and lost family members, and have gone for long periods without adequate food, shelter, or health services (Victorian Settlement Planning Committee, 2006). When they attend school, they will bring all these trauma experiences into their classroom setting.

To meet these challenges, teachers need to be aware of and be responsive to refugee students' backgrounds, levels of their English language fluency, disrupted education for some of them, the pressures of resettlement, racial discrimination, and the possible impact of trauma or war experience on their learning. Teachers should be able to develop their critical understanding of not only cultural diversity but also refugee culture and to apply their understanding of this concept to manage their own classroom.

This raises challenges for teachers who are faced with classes made up of a combination of local and non-local students. Teachers would like to manage diversity by making sure that all students feel comfortable in their classrooms. However, they are not exactly confident about how to achieve this task. Sometimes they want to incorporate the cultural heritages of students into curriculum, but that culture might be considered wrong in their own cultural traditions. They want to use appropriate discipline practices but do not always understand the behaviour of their students.

Therefore, as teachers are responsible for developing proper strategies to help students in learning, they can play a key role in shaping students' views about life and learning in a broader social and historical context by appropriate engagement. This brings to the surface the need for teachers to be more equipped in managing the needs of multicultural students in the classrooms.

Moreover, although the effect of teacher's multicultural competence on classroom management is clear, the dynamics of how a teacher produces such an effect are not simple. Studies investigating cultural competencies in teachers have indicated that teachers feel different degrees of competency in many components of cultural competence.

For instance, teachers perceived high levels of cultural awareness but were unsure about their levels of cultural knowledge and skills. In addition, despite many studies in multicultural classroom management and teacher cultural competence, there is however, no one effective plan which we can apply to make managing classroom with cultural diversity students. It is always a never-ending process when it comes to cultural competency.

Also, Australian schools are continuing to become more and more diverse; therefore, it is important for teachers to improve efficiency of cultural diversity within their classrooms. By re-examining the components of cultural competence that may reinforce classroom management, there is a set of standards for cultural competence that can be used as a point of reference for teachers in multicultural settings; although, different students may require different services to meet their specific needs.

In addition, despite many studies in multicultural classroom management and the teacher's cultural competence, there is however, no effective plan which we can apply to make managing classrooms with cultural diversity students successfully. As the student population in Australian schools becomes increasingly diverse, teachers also need professional development to build cultural competencies: skills, knowledge, and awareness related to issues such as language, culture, and ethnicity in managing multicultural classroom.

> *"A teacher who has been taught throughout elementary and secondary school by respected teachers who used a direct transmission mode*

of delivery and very little student-centred inquiry is likely to identify with that mode of teaching and be deeply resistant to superficial attempts to change. Ignored or neglected, ideas instilled through the apprenticeship of observation can completely sabotage later efforts at formal teacher preparation." (Mendenhall et al., 2021, p. 6).

According to Mendenhall et al. (2021) teachers can play a major role in creating positive learning environments by providing a safe space for thinking and discussing positive discipline and corporal punishment. Positive, inclusive classrooms can only be developed if teachers are agents of change (Mendenhall et al., 2021). But in a world where many immigrant and refugee children are attending mainstream schools, schools and teachers face the challenge of meeting their language and other needs.

As recently published data shows, immigrant, and refugee students from 135 different languages came into Victorian government schools in 2016 (Department of Education and Training, 2017), illustrating the magnitude of the challenge in Victoria, Australia, where this study is situated.

When one considers that these students do not only have limited English proficiency, but it also makes the challenge for schools, teachers, and school systems even greater; they often have low literacy levels in the languages they already speak. Due to traumatic pasts, the students may have acute emotional and well-being needs, along with literacy and academic needs, and not surprisingly, they may exhibit challenging behaviour.

Diverse classrooms have contributed to recent advancements in teacher preparation. Even so, it remains a challenge for teachers to develop their ability to teach low-income and ethnically diverse students. In diverse classrooms, teachers may find it challenging to manage educational, developmental, interactional, and societal demands of learners (Farmer et al., 2019). This makes it essential that future teachers acquire the skills, knowledge, and dispositions they need to deliver quality instruction to multicultural students (Kelly-jackson et al., 2016).

Despite being different from traditional teaching practices, culturally relevant teaching practices can be learned (Powell, Cantrell and Rightmyer, 2013). In this time of accelerating globalisation and internationalisation, people are most likely to encounter diverse cultures at their work, social, and educational institutions.

As the number of students in regular and international primary schools increases in terms of language, culture, ethnicity, talent, and skills, primary school teachers must acquire the necessary competencies to effectively carry out this broader task. Moreover, a globally competent teacher is knowledgeable about global conditions, current events, the interconnectedness and interdependence of the world, and intercultural communication (van Werven et al., 2021).

According to Sue & Sue (2008, cited in Vincent and Torres, 2015) "Multicultural Competence is the ability to engage in activities or build conditions that maximize the potential of individuals or specific systems." An individual achieves this by acquiring the awareness, knowledge, and skills that enable them to function effectively in a diverse society, and on a societal level, by promoting successful development of new theories, policies, practices, and organizational forms that are more likely to be accepted by all groups (Sue, 2001).

An early discussion of the topic was provided by Banks (1995, cited in Vincent and Torres, 2015) who explains the significance of education considering three concepts of multicultural competence. While the first concept, awareness, describes ethnic diversity as a growing societal phenomenon that impacts young people, the second, knowledge, asserts that people receive information, sometimes untrue, about cultural or ethnic groups. According to the third concept, skills, people's attitudes, and knowledge about cultural and ethnic groups restrict their perspectives and negatively affect the opportunities they have.

Sue, Arrendondo, and McDavis (2002, cited in Vincent and Torres, 2015) created a 'Tripartite Model of Multicultural Counselling Competencies' for clarifying the concept of multicultural competence and its impacts on individuals/societies; however, following various issues concerning the integration of psychology, Sue (2001) developed a multidimensional model called 'Model for Developing Cultural Competence (MDCC)'. Multicultural competence includes three main components: cultural/racial perspective, elements of cultural competency, and cultural competence centres. Each cell in the model represents a combination of the three main dimensions.

While the first dimension refers to acknowledging culture or race, the second is composed of the constructs from multicultural counselling competencies: beliefs, knowledge, and skills (Sue et al., 1998, cited in Sue, 2001). In terms of the third dimension of analysis, the individual is compared to (Vincent and Torres, 2015) the organizational approach of analysis. Multicultural competence begins and focuses on the individual level (Sue et al., 1998, cited in Sue, 2001).

According to Martin & Sugarman (1993) classroom management applies to teacher's activities that create a positive classroom climate and as a result, effective teaching and learning will occur. Therefore, teachers, as culturally responsive classroom managers, need to be aware of their own cultural values and biases and reflect on how these affect their expectations about student behaviour, communication with them, and student performance.

Weinstein, Tomlinson-Clarke and Curran (2004, p.27) also suggest a five-part concept of a culturally responsive classroom management framework: "recognition of one's own cultural lens and biases, knowledge of students' cultural backgrounds, awareness of the broader social, economic and political context, ability and willingness to use culturally appropriate management strategies, and comm tment to building caring classroom communities" and this framework can be considered as a main technique in cultural classroom management.

Besides, there is broad research on traditional classroom management and culturally responsive pedagogy which focuses on curriculum content and teaching strategies but doesn't really focus on the issue of management that teachers who lack cultural competence often experience problems in this area.

Cultural Competence is an appropriate approach to running classrooms with all children in a culturally responsive way and guides the management decisions that teachers make. Booysen (2003, p.24) states "to survive the challenges of educational change and to be successful, educational leaders need to become competent in managing multicultural education".

As teachers become more effective in their teaching, it becomes necessary for them to have the appropriate management skills, acknowledge cultural differences that will place them in a position to understand diverse learners, and be sensitive to individuals around stereotyped differences.

Intercultural Awareness vs. Intercultural Empathy

Intercultural awareness can be considered as the foundation of communication. It includes two qualities: first is the awareness of one's own culture; the second is the awareness of other culture. It includes the ability of standing back from one's own point and becoming aware of other cultures values, perceptions and believes. Cultural awareness becomes crucial when individuals communicate with individual from other culture. It avoids misunderstanding when people communicate.

4

Teachers' Intercultural Competence

Now and after introducing cultural competence and its importance in managing diverse primary classrooms this chapter will highlight the role of competent teachers in managing diversity. Intercultural communicative competence (ICC) will be defined and a comparison between (ICC) and (IC) which is essential in a world that is unstable and diverse will be drawn.

This chapter will show the imperative for the modern personality to develop intercultural competence (ICC), as well as improving work efficiency.

Intercultural Communicative Competence (ICC)

Before proceeding into the intercultural communitive competence let's see what cultural competence and what is intercultural competence, and why it is important for teacher education. According to Laird S (2013) individuals and systems need to be culturally competent to deal with people of all cultures, languages, classes, races, ethnic backgrounds, religions, spiritual traditions, immigration status, and other diversity factors respectfully and effectively. To recognize, affirm, and value everyone, family, and community and protect and preserve the dignity of everyone, family, and community.

The term "cultural competence" refers to a set of behaviours, attitudes, and policies that enable organizations, systems, or professional groups to work effectively across cultures. The concept of cultural competence can be defined operationally as integrating and transforming knowledge about individuals and groups into specific standards, policies, practices, and attitudes for use in appropriate cultural settings to improve the quality of services (Laird S, 2013). While intercultural competence has been described by hundreds of characteristics (Deardorff, 2004).

In the context of research on intercultural competence, several authors discuss communication, conflict resolution, empathy, awareness of ethnic stereotypes, and identifying intercultural similarities and differences, including non-verbal communication (John O. Summers, 2001; Deardorff, 2006; Schelfhout et al., 2022; Novikova et al., 2022).

Intercultural competence (IC) is the ability of foreign language learners to communicate in their own language with people from other cultures and countries. They must develop their understanding of intercultural communication, attitudes towards otherness, and interpreting, relating, and discovering skills to accomplish this (Byram 1997, cited in Tashmatova, 2021). Thus, intercultural communicative competence (ICC) becomes essential to interact with other people (Dimitrova-gyuzeleva, 2019).

Intercultural communicative competence involves the ability to interact with other people, but this interaction takes place in a foreign language between people from different cultures and countries according to (Dimitrova-gyuzeleva, 2019). It is through their ability to use language appropriately as well as their awareness of the specific meaning, values, and connotations of the language that participants of another culture have knowledge of their culture. Moreover, linguistic competence, sociolinguistic competence, discourse competence, and intercultural competence are all included in ICC (Tashmatova, 2021).

Scholars and researchers have identified the concept of intercultural communicative competence. There is a valuable variety of definitions for ICC in the literature, but basically it is defined as; intercultural communicative competence (ICC) refers to the "capacity to ensure a shared understanding between people of different social identities, as well as the ability to interact with people as complex human beings with multiple identities and their own uniqueness (Sandra et al., 2016). According to Deardorff (2004), ICC is the ability to communicate effectively in intercultural situations based on one's intercultural skills, knowledge, and attitudes.

Based on Byram's (1997) model of ICC, there are three main factors: Knowledge of the social group and its products and practices is the first factor. The second factor is skills: the skill of interpreting, the skill of relating, and the skill of discovering, which all together assist individuals in learning, explaining, and comparing the meaning of a given situation or document from another culture.

As a third element of ICC, one needs to be open-minded, empathy-oriented, ready to learn and curious about cultural expressions that might be similar or quite different from their own. Byram (1997) suggests that learners can acquire another savoir - critical cultural awareness - with knowledge, skills, and attitudes. This savoir allows them to analyse critically the differences and dynamics between our own culture and the target culture, since human beings do not behave and think similarly, but act and see the world differently (Fernando and Rodríguez, 2013). Once empathy is modelled, practiced, and discussed during teacher preparation, it is an essential tool a teacher candidate can use to gain a deeper understanding of the culture of students (Warren, 2018). It is therefore through learning cultures that learners can reflect on what they have learned, contemplate on their ideas, and develop their skills and practices through these activities (Huda et al., 2017).

Further, according to Dimitrova-gyuzeleva (2019) achieving effective intercultural communication requires:

» **EMPATHY**: Understanding another's behaviour and thoughts.
» **RESPECT**: Appreciation of different ways of thinking and communicating.
» **TOLERANT**: The ability and willingness to accept and acknowledge different behaviours, attitudes, and opinions that do not necessarily align with one's own.
» **SENSITIVITY**: Being aware and responsive to the actions and ideas of others.
» **FLEXIBILITY**: Openness to change and openness to alternative ways of thinking.

Focus on empathy is due to the incredible claims it has been made for its redemptive powers, including its use as a tool for social justice, as well as the strong expectation among many teacher educators that empathy should be taught and enhanced (Jordan, 2019). There are at least two functions of empathy in teacher education.

As a first step, empathic teacher educators can use empathy to help teacher candidates notice patterns in their own attitudes, beliefs, and values regarding race and culture. The second reason is that, once empathy is modelled, practiced, and discussed during teacher preparation, it is an essential tool a teacher candidate can use to gain a deeper understanding of the culture of students (Warren, 2018). Empathy, curiosity, and respect for other cultures are also essential (Arasaratnam and Doerfel, 2005; Deardorff 2006b).

Teachers' Intercultural Competence

To become culturally competent, three factors must be present: attitude, skills, and knowledge. To support this perspective, Hofstede (2001, cited in Johnson, Lenartowicz and Apud, 2006) proposes an awareness, knowledge, and skill-based process of intercultural communication competence. He suggests that individuals can attain intercultural competence by learning it, but that personality factors also play a role. The authors suggest that to become culturally competent, an individual must:

1) Possess a strong sense of identity.

2) Understanding the culture's values and beliefs; Demonstrate an understanding of cultural affective processes.

3) Clear communication in each cultural group's language.

4) Engage in special behaviours that are sanctioned.

5) Maintain active social relationships within the cultural community.

6) The institutional structures of that culture must be negotiated (Johnson, Lenartowicz and Apud, 2006).

The Importance of Interculturally Competent Teachers

A world that is unstable and diverse makes it imperative for the modern personality to develop intercultural competence (ICC), as well as improving work efficiency. Intercultural competence (ICC) is crucial for obtaining education and establishing social bonds, that is, for solving important problems for adults and children, starting from a very young age. Increasing globalization and migration processes have resulted in children of different nationalities and ethnicities studying together more and more often in the school classroom.

Cultural differences in interaction tend to result in improved academic performance and cognitive abilities in school students who take this into account and accept them (Novikova et al., 2022). A Ministerial Group and the Australian Government announced early in 2015 that 'urgent national action is needed to improve teacher education quality'. The Australian government responded by reforming teacher education, focusing on 'quality teachers' and 'classroom readiness'. Designed around a logic of deficiency within initial teacher education, the reforms mandate accreditation processes, standard assessment procedures, and the National Literacy and Numeracy Test for pre-service teachers. Regardless of the quality of the course and intentions of lecturers, the job of a teacher is to mentor his/her students on a culturally responsive level through the learning phase. Teachers can have a rich understanding of students with "understanding their history as oppressed groups, their cultural frames of reference, and their everyday social practices".

Personal reflections of identity are a good starting point for pre-service teachers to develop an understanding of their students' diversity. That means they develop an awareness of themselves as cultural beings, and to see themselves as part of the entire multicultural, rather than outside of it. Tartakover (2013) by researching on cultural identity in pre-service teachers concluded that before being able to start thinking about developing an inclusive pedagogy, teachers must have the belief that diversity is a positive characteristic. She mentioned that still some of the participants did not feel as prepared as they would have liked to in adopting culturally responsive pedagogy.

Further, it is important of placement experiences with mentor teachers who are effective in teaching culturally diverse learners and the ongoing guidance and support pre-service teachers. Besides, teacher education courses need to instil in pre-service teachers a commitment to ongoing learning, which includes researching about different cultures and their histories. According to Tartakover (2013) new teachers agreed that the most significant factors encouraging new teachers' abilities to incorporate social justice into their practice are support, professional respect, and the freedom to explore new ways of teaching in a way that is responsive to the culture of the students' population. Therefore, culturally competent teachers assure that the curriculum will be taught, and their students will not only learn the coursework, but will be grown as individuals.

Teacher Training in Intercultural Education

As teacher education programs face the challenges of educating teachers about diversity, diversity-focused courses (such as multicultural education, urban education, and teaching English language learners) have become part of their curriculums, as well as placements in diverse schools and communities. By adding diversity-focused courses and emphasizing the need for collaboration with communities, teacher education students will have more opportunities to interact with diverse communities.

Many teacher education students grew up in communities that differ from the mainstream, based on their social class, race, and ethnicity, and primary language (Yuan, 2017). Intercultural education provides a holistic view of the integration process of immigrants. Mutual respect, exchange, cooperation, and peaceful coexistence between people from diverse cultures are the pillars of it. Due to this, teacher training programs related to diversity have grown in recent years.

The training of teachers for cultural diversity cannot be based on commitments of certain departments or areas but must be formulated by the trainers who are responsible for such training in a coordinated manner. It is an interdisciplinary process, in which the various didactics, together with the other fields of knowledge, reinforce their commitment to the inclusion of cultural diversity as an important part of the learning to teach process (Figueredo-Canosa et al., 2020).

Teacher Continuous Professional Development for Inclusion

> *"A teacher who has been taught throughout elementary and secondary school by respected teachers who used a direct transmission mode of delivery and very little student-centred inquiry is likely to identify with that mode of teaching and be deeply resistant to superficial attempts to change. Ignored or neglected, ideas instilled through the apprenticeship of obser- vation can completely sabotage later efforts at formal teacher preparation". (Schwille, Dembélé, and Schubert 2007, cited in Mendenhall et al., 2021).*

Teaching in diverse classes with learners having a variety of needs can be challenging for teachers (Farmer et al., 2019). From Farmers' et al., perspective all students can benefit from contact w th peers who are different in different ways, and social integration within the classroom is crucial to students' school success. To support the social adaptation of diverse students, teachers must understand classroom dynamics. It is also necessary for teachers to deve op strategies that promote engaged classroom climates and leverage positive peer dynamics.

According to their review, peer relations and social adjustment are analysed from a person-in-context perspective, specifically in classrooms with a variety of student characteristics and instructional needs. Using social dynamics management strategies, teachers can create classroom communities that promote student involvement and adjustment.

Most students in American schools for example are culturally, linguistically, and academically heterogeneous. A number of requirements must be met by states receiving federal education funds under the Education of Students with Disabilities Act : (1) the importance of educating students with disabilities alongside their peers without disabilities was stressed, (2) encouraging students with disabilities to access and engage with general education curriculum to improve their academic outcomes, and (3) a positive behavioural support program was needed to reduce discipline issues also to prevent exclusion or removal of learners with disabilities from their proper educational position due to their behaviour issues.

It could be said that a student's academic and behavioural success is tied to how the student feels about the teacher and their perception of how the teacher feels about them. The quality of the teacher–pupil relationship, when characterized by closeness, affection, and support, can contribute to the development of a child and to his/her adaptation to the school context in a positive way.

According to Longobardi et al. (2021) there is an association between closeness in student–teacher relationships and several outcomes, (i.e., academic competence, attitude towards school, and prosocial behaviour). Research suggests that a child's prosocial behavior increases when he or she has a close relationship with their teacher (Longobardi et al., 2021). Prosocial behaviour may be positively correlated with empathy. In fact, this kind of relationship characterized by closeness, which is perceived both by the teacher and by the pupil, is positively associated with higher level of prosocial behaviour in the child (Longobardi et al., 2021).

The issue then is not what is being taught, but how it is received by students that are culturally diverse. Students attending the same school and taking the same classes can have a completely different educational experience.

Some students may feel that certain teachers do not like them and therefore be less willing to work to the classroom standards. Yet, these same students will work well with other teachers. Again, as DuPraw and Axner (1997) asserts on how to act culturally competent and be aware of the power imbalances, thus, it is critical to consider avoiding the power relations (authority) of teachers in diverse classrooms such as Victorian/Australian context.

Authority is a central issue for teachers and refers to the leadership relationship between teachers and pupils for the purpose of initiating learning. A review of the current state of research shows that the interplay between authority and social inequality has seldom been investigated to date. That is the starting point for Weitkämper's (2022) ethnographic research project. It adopts a sociological and socio-philosophical perspective on the relevance of social background in negotiations of authority between pupils and teachers in inclusive primary schools in Germany. With respect to the developed concept of un/doing authority, it shows that the aspect of vulnerability is particularly important in these interactions.

The study comes to the following conclusion: the mutual vulnerability of "good" pupils and teachers is recognised, whereas teachers' relationships with "bad" pupils show a mutual violation that can often be understood as a re-enactment of social inequalities and future educational exclusion (Weitkämper, 2022).

Frameworks for Teacher Competency

According to Halász (2019) it is important for modern societies to regulate professional activities and professions through competency frameworks. The concept of competency frameworks refers to tools for defining and specifying how individuals working within an organization or team should behave to achieve a common vision or goal (Esser et al., 2018). By using them, professionals can guarantee and enhance their work quality, communication with society, and client satisfaction, and orient their professional development (Madlinske, 2018).

Professionals are distinguished from non-professionals by their ability to perform an essential social function; the acquisition of specialized knowledge and skills that are useful in solving complex problems; and their commitment to professional ethics, developed through a period of professional socialization; A high level of prestige and financial compensation; and the freedom to make decisions and recommendations as a professional in practice.

As professional accrediting and regulating bodies adopt, adapt, and develop their entry to-practice competence frameworks, higher/tertiary education programs must transform their educational programs to become increasingly competency-based (Rich, 2019). By ensuring and improving professionalism in the workplace, communicating society's demands to professionals, orienting professional development, and supporting ethical behaviour, professional work can be improved and ensured by them. Teacher policies also use these powerful tools to improve teachers' performance. Qualification frameworks based on competency descriptions encourage their use as quality improvement tools (Halász, 2019).

Several emerging frameworks provide educators with useful steps that can be taken to develop cultural competence and racial awareness. Duncan-Andrade (2008) offers five core pillars of racial and cultural competence for teachers of culturally diverse students: (1) critically conscious purpose, where teachers ask, "Why do I teach?" and "Whom do I teach?" and have clear and realistic answers to these questions; (2) duty, in which teachers have a commitment to the com- munities and students that they teach; (3) preparation, which entails teachers having solid classroom management skills and giving intense commitment and time to their curricular decision making, lesson planning, and assessment; (4) Socratic sensibility, or teachers' ability to find a balance between their confidence as teachers and their ability to engage in frequent self-critique; and (5) trust, or the building of authentic relationships between students and teachers in ways that are predicated on mutual levels of trust and respect.

The European Commission for instance has proposed using competence frameworks to "boost teacher quality" as part of a recent study (European Commission, 2018). Integrated policy mixes for improving teacher quality in education systems were assumed to include them as a core component.

Likewise, researchers from Russia and abroad note that young teachers' professional activities are hindered by the inability to apply theoretical knowledge in practice in the context of university studies. With the competence approach implemented in Russia's education system today, this problem can be solved through the development of special, general, and key competencies. The professional competence of primary school teachers includes a variety of private methodological competencies as well. Language and methodological competence are one of these competencies that ensures a teacher is prepared to teach the Russian language to primary school students (Khairova and Zakirova, 2019). Therefore, it is important for modern societies to regulate professional activities and professions through competency frameworks.

Developing Disciplinary Literacy in Pre-Service Teachers

Over the last few decades, teacher identity research has grown substantially, resulting in a substantial body of literature, but fewer studies have examined professional identity development in specific settings, and there are fewer studies that relate directly to science teachers' identities as literacy teachers (Ollerhead, 2020). Ollerhead looked to other disciplines for insight into the development of professional teacher identity as the acquisition of other domains of knowledge, drawing upon the work of (Bennison, 2016) who proposes a framework for developing the professional identity of an in-service history teacher as a numeracy embedder. According to Bennison's framework, professional identity development is affected by five interconnected domains, namely knowledge, affect, social, life history, and context. A focus on the characteristics that are especially relevant to a teacher who provides opportunities for students' numeracy development is placed within each of these domains. As 'embedders of literacy', PSTs develop similar identities in such domains.

In an undergraduate PST education programme at an Australian university, Ollerhead has conducted previous research into the emerging literacy knowledge of science PSTs. It concluded that teachers developed their professional identities in this way by becoming increasingly aware of the fact that effective science teachers must do more than master the curriculum content to succeed. Rather, it demanded they consider how best to teach this content, including addressing the language and literacy skills required to interact with the content. Teachers' values influenced their choices of content, textbook use, pedagogical strategies, and perceptions of students' needs (Spector, 2015).

A significant way Australia recognizes the needs of its multilingual learners is through preservice teacher training (PST) (Ollerhead, 2020). According to Hammond (2014) many mainstream secondary school teachers feel inadequately prepared to meet the complex language and literacy challenges faced by EAL learners. As a result, most universities are developing more targeted language and literacy programs for preservice student teachers (PSTs), giving them in-field training that exposes them to addressing language and literacy demands in different learning areas and observing and reflecting about the impact they have on the learning of students. Teachers' professional identities are affected by such programs.

Teachers should see themselves as teachers of literacy as well as teachers of their own disciplines if they are to support literacy across the curriculum. Their professional identities as literacy teachers must be developed. To support PSTs in this endeavour, teacher education programmes must consider how professional identities are developed (Ollerhead, 2020).

The Need for Teacher Training in Australia

For social justice and multiculturalism to be taken seriously, the teacher population must reflect the growing diversity of society and intercultural communication studies should be included in the professional training curriculum for future teachers (Havrilova et al.,

2021). A teacher should possess a sense of mission, solidarity with, and empathy for their students, as well as the courage to challenge mainstream knowledge, improvisational skills, and a passion for social justice (Bhopal and Rhamie, 2014). The experiences and histories of teachers play a significant role in shaping their identities as teachers. The process of becoming a teacher is shaped by experiences of failure, however little is known about how they influence that process. The importance of gaining this insight, however, can be further undermined if failure defines teachers and their work (Lutovac and Assunção Flores, 2021).

According to Ollerhead (2020) recently, Australian schools have become increasingly multilingual, with students needing linguistic and cultural resources in addition to academic English support. A critical role for preservice teacher training is to identify and describe the language and literacy demands in all disciplines, according to policymakers. It is now widely recognized that merely immersing multilingual EAL students in English content classrooms is not enough to enable them to develop their language, literacy, or academic skills (Hammond, 2014.)

Even though most EAL learners develop conversational English relatively quickly, mastering academic language takes at least five years, and often substantially longer. There are many technical and low-frequency words specific to specific content areas, as well as increasingly complex grammar, like passive voice, which is rarely used in social conversations (Collier, 1987). There has been a growing recognition by some educators (e.g., Norris and Phillips, 2003) that students need to be able to interpret and construct representations of scientific concepts, processes, claims, and findings.

Researchers have reconceptualised science as a process of acquiring disciplinary literacy (Osborne, 2007; Moje, 2007; Norris and Phillips, 2003). To really understand science, rather than simply 'knowing about' it, Phillips (2003) argue that students must be able to interpret, represent, and assess scientific claims, all of which rely on linguistic representations. For students to explore and investigate the natural world, they need literacies that support their exploration and investigation. In addition to comprehending and composing texts, they must be able to comprehend and compose pictures, maps, animations, models, and visual media. A strong understanding of language structures is also necessary for students to link information and ideas, provide descriptions and explanations, and formulate hypotheses and arguments based on evidence (Ollerhead, 2020).

5

Significance of Empathy in Education

Empathy will be defined in this chapter. Types of empathy: cognitive and affective empathy are scrutinized. Benefits of empathy in lowering the risk of prejudice development are also explored specifically reducing or preventing school problems, as well as improving a classroom teacher's ability to respond to culturally responsive pedagogies.

Empathy

Empathy is a Greek word "empatheia", that means understanding others by "standing in somebody else's shoes" or entering their world. Empathy refers to the ability for one person to understand the internal emotional circumstances of another (Rodriguez et al., 2021). Davis (1983) stated that empathy is understood as a response based on observing experiences of others. A common definition of empathy is the ability to read and feel (affective) our ability to understand and predict the intentions of others based on their intellectual states (Overgaauw et al., 2014). In addition, empathy arises from and is affected by another's emotional arousal and state (Zaki, Bolger and Ochsner, 2009). Pionke and Graham, (2021) define empathy as a feeling of understanding between two people.

However, the definition of empathy is debated because it can encompass a wide range of actions, from feelings to social behaviours. Moreover, David 1994 cited in (Anderson and Shannon, 1988) sees empathy as a multidimensional phenomenon that involves feeling similar feelings as the other, having feelings of empathic concern, and understanding the other. However, empathy is not an exclusive phenomenon, meaning all or nothing, but rather is made up of a variety of forms and intensities of showing and experiencing empathy, ranging from simply feeling their pain to fully understanding them and foreseeing the eventual outcome.

While observing another individual's emotional, psychological, or physical condition, it is the internal resonance or "inner imitation" that a person experiences. Empathy is defined as the ability to realize another's feelings (Cognitive empathy), feeling of emotional response that is coherent with other individuals' emotional states (Affective empathy) (Cohen & Strayer, 1996; Davis, 1996, cited in López-Pérez et al., 2017).

Empathy is generally defined as the capacity of perceiving the feeling state of another and the consequences of doing so accurately (Spreng et al., 2009). As a means of allowing another person to feel understood, empathy is defined as feeling liked and understood by the other person (Magid and Shane, 2017). Ziv, Golbez and Shapira (2020) describe empathy as a construct comprising four emotional and cognitive dimensions: perspective taking (Ability to naturally adopt other people's perspectives), fantasy (Identification with characters in unreal situations), empathic concern (Compassion, warmth, and concern for others), as well as personal distress (A feeling of discomfort, anxiety, and helplessness when a critical emotional situation arises, e.g., an emergency).

Human empathy is defined by (Tabullo, Navas Jiménez and Silvana Garcia, 2018) as understanding others' thoughts, feelings, and intentions in each situation by adopting the other person's perspective. Empathy is a multidimensional phenomenon comprised of cognitive, affective, moral, and behavioural aspects (Ratka, 2018).

Types of Empathy

There are two main components of empathy that can be distinguished: cognitive (understanding the feelings and thoughts of another individual and the ability to perceive their perspective), and affective component (a witness's proper emotional experience and the ability to react to another individual's emotional state). Researchers have identified two types of empathy: affective and cognitive.

Affective empathy is the experience of feeling another's emotions. The affective aspect of empathy can be defined as the ability to share and experience emotions with others (Coskun, 2019).

To be cognitively empathic means to understand and identify other people's emotions. A person who has empathy can understand and identify situations, motives, feelings, and perspectives, as well as recognize and appreciate concerns of others; they are curious about strangers, discover commonalities and challenge prejudice, open up to others, listen, inspire social change, and develop an ambitious imagination (Ratka, 2018).

In the phenomenological tradition, empathy was viewed as an experiential act sui generis that is not theoretical or inferential, analogous to perception. Individuals can directly grasp the experiences of other people by seeing their movements without necessarily experiencing similar experiences themselves (Bevir and Stueber, 2011).

Theories of empathy describe it as a multidimensional construct integrating: 1) automatic affective experiences of observed emotional states, and 2) understanding of others' thoughts and feelings through controlled cognitive processes. Thus, most current theoretical models distinguish between two aspects of empathy: cognitive empathy, which is interpreting, representing, understanding, and separating beliefs, intentions, feelings, and emotions of others from our own, and affective empathy, which is being able to feel affective reactions to what others are experiencing.

A crucial distinction between cognitive and affective empathy is that cognitive empathy involves the representation of the affective state from another person's perspective, whereas affective empathy involves experiencing and appropriating the feelings, at least on a gross level (Tabullo, Navas Jiménez and Silvana García, 2018).

Benefits of Empathy

The ability to empathize is a critical element of morality (Masto, 2015). We reflect on others' feelings when we are empathic. In order to achieve ideal communication, one should understand how the other thinks and behaves (Zhu, 2011). As we empathize with others, we have a regulatory system that can counter possible overacting resulting from this empathetic response (Overgaauw et al., 2014).

Prejudice is rooted in empathy (Rutland and Killen, 2015). There is research evidence that shows a relationship between empathy and prejudice in children, teenagers, and adults were studied (Miklikowska, 2018). Various studies support the benefits of empathy as a factor in fostering positive attitudes towards diverse groups. It has been demonstrated that empathizing with each member of the diverse group (i.e., experiencing sympathy and compassion for that individual) can lead to increased care for that individual.

Insofar as the member is representative of the outgroup, this increased caring extends to the outgroup and is manifested both as more positive attitudes towards, and greater support for, behavioural actions that assist the outgroup. Therefore, increases in empathy should lower the risk of prejudice development.

Although empathy has a cognitive aspect rather than being purely emotional, still it is an affecting concept, and conceptualizing emotions in others is a talent full of cognitions (Zaki, Bolger and Ochsner, 2009). In general, empathy consists of understanding and experiencing what others feel in terms of emotion and sensation.

Also, for Bennett (1998), empathy facilitates imagining another person's perspective (not agreeing with or adopting his or her views) (Drewelow and Finney, 2020). An empathic person is able to respond and identify with the mental and emotional states of others, including the ability to comprehend and recognize their emotions (Meng et al., 2021).

People who show empathy can empathize with others, adapt to their colleagues, respond in a timely manner to the problems of loved ones and show sensitivity (Syse, 2020). In classrooms context the ability to empathize with students and establish productive student-teacher relationships is considered critical to academic success Warren (2015). Empathy facilitates risk-taking and instructional flexibility, fosters trust between students and teachers, and assists teachers' ability to intervene proactively to ensure that students meet high academic standards (Warren, 2013). Also, by developing empathy skills, school problems may be reduced or prevented (Kokkinos and Kipritsi, 2018).

Besides, in regard to physicians and patients they benefit from clinical empathy by improving accurate diagnosis and treatment, increasing patient satisfaction and compliance, and lowering burnout and stress (Assing Hvidt et al., 2020). Thus, empathy is a crucial element of normal social functioning.

> *"Empathy motivates helping others and the desire to do so as well as inhibits aggression, facilitates social competence, and provides a sense of connection among people" (Zhou et al., 2003, cited in Tettegah & Anderson, 2007).*

Besides, it has been determined that empathy improves a classroom teacher's ability to (re)act or respond to youth in ways that result in CRP (Warren, 2018). In multicultural and urban classrooms, teachers are believed to develop their teaching efficiency through empathy (Warren, 2014).

However, there are few models that are useful for training and preparing teachers to develop empathy as a professional skill (Banks 2007; Banks and Banks 2010 cite in Warren,2014). Teachers' ability to fulfill their professional roles successfully may be influenced by empathy (Stojiljković, Djigić and Zlatković, 2012). Empathy allows us to perceive similarities between ourselves and outgroups (Miklikowska, 2018).

Teachers' Empathy

A teacher's professional training should emphasize empathy in order to teach in diverse school contexts (Tettegah and Anderson, 2007). Supervisors of teacher candidates should develop it (Warren, 2014). Researchers recently concluded that empathic nature is a professional feature of active teachers in urban settings (Gordon 1999 cited in Warren, 2015). Students of colour would probably benefit from its application if they are using it in the classroom (Warren, 2014).

Teachers' empathy is thought to be crucial to the success of multicultural classrooms (Dolby, 2012; Floward, 2010; Ladson-Billings, 2006; McAllister & Irvine, 2002;

Milner, 2010 cited in Warren, 2015). A variety of models of empathy studies across disciplines have revealed that a teacher's empathic capabilities can improve different student outcomes (Tettegah, 2005; Tettegah and Anderson, 2007). When a teacher demonstrates empathy, they deliberately use their knowledge about the student to create relationships that are meaningful to the student. It also includes students demonstrating concerns and being vulnerable about issues that concern them.

Incorporating Empathy into Education and Teaching

Empathy has been incorporated into education and teaching. Having empathy means taking on the perspective of students, including those from other cultures, and responding to them from that perspective (McAllister and Irvine, 2002). Furthermore, it refers to the facilitator's ability to understand and re-experience the student's feelings.

Relationship building involves questioning and listening to students' viewpoints to better understand their viewpoints and feelings on various topics in the classroom and SEL programming. Empathy is critical for increasing academic outcomes and building positive relationships between teachers and students (Warren, 2015). The ability to respond to adolescents in ways that show evidence of cultural responsive pedagogies (CRP) has been found to be enhanced by empathy (Warren,

2018). Educators' efforts to convey care to students include empathizing with them (Warren, 2015). By developing empathy skills, school problems may be reduced or prevented (Kokkinos and Kipritsi, 2018).

As empathy is the ability to understand others' emotional states and respond to them in a socially beneficial manner (Lee, Lee and Kim, 2018), thus, students who understand and respond to other students' or teachers' feelings at school are more likely to be satisfied with their schools (Kokkinos and Kipritsi, 2018).

Conceptualizing Empathy

There are several different ways to conceptualize empathy in different theoretical models. According to Davis (1983) the concept of empathy can be described as the reaction to observing the experiences of others. Further, empathy is a state triggered and affected by another's emotional arousal and state.

Empathy has been addressed by its affective aspect as a skill to share and experience emotions with others (Coskun, 2019). The concept of empathy is a highly complex concept, essential for successful and fulfilling social interactions since it determines whether an individual's reactions to others' emotional states are appropriate.

Knowing from a Personal Perspective

A social interaction begins when an observer observes a target in a risky situation that requires intervention by the observer, according to social psychology. An imagined self (IS) is when an observer responds to a target's situation or condition based on personal experience/ preference, or a conceptualization or construction of the observer in the target's place (Warren, 2018).

Empathetic people accurately communicate their thoughts, understand the sentiments of others in challenging circumstances, and act accordingly. Associating with others, providing care for their well-being, and cooperating among group members rely on empathy in interpersonal relations.

There are numerous perspectives offered by the field of social psychology (Davis, 1994; Eisenberg & Strayer, 1987, cited in Warren, 2015) for understanding how human beings enact and develop empathetic dispositions. During childhood into adulthood, the ability to empathize with others, particularly strangers, becomes more sophisticated and requires more effort. When empathizing, individuals' life experiences and backgrounds contribute to interactions that affect their ability to empathize (Warren, 2015).

6

Intercultural Empathetic Competence

This chapter will introduce intercultural empathetic competencies that will help teachers who are working in multicultural classrooms how to develop their professional skills. Since students in Australian schools are becoming increasingly diverse, teachers must develop cultural competencies; the ability to recognize, understand, and identify issues such as culture, ethnicity, and language. By having empathy this will facilitate teachers' ability to take risks and be flexible with instruction, creates trusting relationships with students, and supports teachers' ability to intervene proactively to ensure that students meet high academic standards.

Significance of Empathy to Intercultural Classroom Practice

In a classroom context having empathy facilitates teachers' ability to take risks and be flexible with instruction, creates trusting relationships with students, and supports teachers' ability to intervene proactively to ensure that students meet high academic standards. Because racial bias on a personal level is the main barrier to education (Yared, Grové and Chapman, 2020), efficacy or effectiveness of interventions including secular contemplative practices for children is needed (Poehlmann-Tynan et al., 2016), in order to foster cooperation and citizenship (Lee, Lee and Kim, 2018).

In regard to race, the primary school years are considered a pivotal period in students' cognitive development (Rutland and Killen, 2015). This is where the child's conception of the world around them begins, and where they find themselves in it. The racism and racial bias that are evident in adults does not manifest in adulthood.Beginning in childhood, it slowly expands throughout life, and by adulthood becomes deeply ingrained and resistant to change (Rutland and Killen 2015). Besides, the development of social-cognitive abilities in children can result in prejudices emerging simultaneously (Aboud et al., 2012).

Additionally, a child's negative views about ethnicity and race can also be formed, (Rutland and Killen 2015), as well as their sense of morality (Yared, Grové and Chapman,

2020). Students need education in policy analysis, budgeting, research methods, and program evaluation. A student also needs "harder skills," for example cultural competence (Blessett, 2018), communicating across boundaries such as gender (Elias & D'Agostino, 2019), and empathy (Edlins and Dolamore, 2018).

The categories of race (Blessett, 2018), socio-economic status ethnicity, nationality, religion, sexual orientation, and disability also fall into the categories of social identity. (National Association of Schools of Public Affairs & Administration [NASPAA], 2006). A student's ability to deal with ambiguity, contradictions, and multiple perspectives is also important. Those issues must be addressed because, if we ignore these issues, inequities will persist, and oppressive systems will persist.

A K-12 setting can benefit from empathy-based instruction (Lee et al. 2018). The development of formal guidelines and best practices regarding empathic design can benefit K-12 education. These guidelines and best practices are applicable across school systems and countries that maintain an empathic, active, and experiential design approach (Dienenthaler et al., 2017, cited in Keahey, 2021).

As educational institutions move towards digital delivery, an empathic approach to instructional design provides a continuous and reflective model for developing learning tools (Keahey, 2021). Hence, having empathy eases educators' ability to be flexible with instructions, creates trusting relationships with students and supports teachers' ability to intervene proactively to ensure that students meet high academic standards.

The Epistemology of Empathy

A general theory of person developed by John Heron (1992, cite in Kasl and Yorks, 2016) is embedded in our analysis of the epistemology of empathy. In Heron's extended epistemology, there are four ways of knowing: experiential, presentational, propositional, and practical. From embodied resonance with phenomena, experiential knowledge is derived; it is prelinguistic, affective, and tacit.

Stories, artistic forms, and metaphors provide expression for presentational knowing, which is an intuitive grasp of imaginal patterns. Evidence-based propositional knowing is expressed in intellectual concepts rooted in logic and based on observable evidence. Practical knowledge leads to competent action.

In adult education literature, Heron's theory accounts for multiple ways of knowing: emotions, embodiment, spirituality, imagination, intuition, analysis, reflection, and action are all incorporated into one of the four ways of knowing as described by Heron.

Concepts are being developed by empathy researchers onto Heron's (1992) model of extended epistemology:

the relationship between empathy and the three tenets of adult learning, as well as the power of presentational knowledge to generate empathy amid diversity. Based on Heron's (1992) epistemology, emotional empathy is a construct located in experiential knowledge. An experiential understanding of emotions and embodiment can be found in direct phenomenological encounters that are tacit and non-linguistic in this instance, a direct encounter with the other and the other's emotions (Kasl and Yorks, 2016).

Moreover, imaginative resistance reveals the central epistemic importance empathy plays for understanding rational agents in a context in which we try to make sense of the moral appropriateness of their reasons for acting (Stueber, 2011). From the teacher's perspective, empathy in early childhood education is the ability to physically feel what the children are feeling, understand why they are feeling that way, and then respond appropriately in response to their needs (Peck, Maude and Brotherson, 2015).

Empathy as Social Necessity.

Empathy is critically important to collaborative and inclusive systems and approaches in a democratic society. It is by and through empathy that individuals can develop shared experiences that create environments of inclusivity and tolerance for diverse experiences and perspectives. Associating with others through it is a social bridge. Children thrive in learning environments where their opinions and perspectives are respected. Creating empathetic classrooms may yield immediate outcomes for improved self-esteem, motivation, and academic performance (Casale and Simmons, 2018).

Empathy and Discomfort as Pedagogies in Multicultural Teacher Education

The combination of discomfort and empathy may be an effective pedagogical strategy in multicultural and antiracist teacher education. It is important to figure out the ways in which discomfort and empathy might be employed together to identify how those practices might be fruitful and strategic for encouraging teachers to change their beliefs and practices as they pertain to antiracist and multicultural education.

The process of changing teachers' attitudes and beliefs is long, difficult, and frequently emotionally painful. However, the combination of discomfort with empathy may offer important openings for antiracist and multicultural teacher education (Zembylas and Papamichael, 2017).

Hence, to teach a learner empathetic ability, as opposed to merely teaching him/her about empathy, requires engaging the learner's attention in their own and others' affective lives. The ability to "feel with" anyone is as much a corporeal achievement as a cerebral one, so the delicate challenge is to facilitate the learners' increased ability to balance their own needs and those of others. The empathetic communicators continuously coordinate their own and another's subjective realities by using their awareness of their own emotional reasoning to gain insight into the other's experience as they are experiencing it.

Empathetic education is not like learning math, acquiring literacy, participating in athletics, or performing in the arts, although some skills and aptitudes associated with each of these kinds of learning overlap with empathetic education. Empathetic communication, on the other hand, aims to achieve a world that exists between and among us, and only then when we participate in creating it.

Cultural/Intercultural Empathy

Cultural empathy is a bridge to integrate the contradictory and disparate elements of cultural competency curriculum to prepare psychotherapists to practice with ethnic populations, therefore, cultural empathy has been proposed. It is significant to be culturally empathic (Grant & Hill, 2020). It is essential for effective cultural communication.

Cultural empathy must be distinguished from sympathy for, identification with, or agreement with a specific culture. However, it is the correct understanding of culture's beliefs and values that matters. In addition, intercultural empathy helps individuals achieve good intercultural communication and build a smooth relation-ship. Individuals often display a range of differences in their ability to empathise when communicating interculturally.

Knowing about others' and own cultures and deliberately shifting into other cultures, they can empathize to understand and be understood across cultural boundaries (Zhu, 2011; Zembylas and Papamichael, 2017). Cross-cultural empathy is a concept that makes cultural sensitivity more coherent. Developing this capacity prepares therapists to practice psychotherapy with diverse clients.

Intercultural empathy includes a variety of problems, such as how to negotiate with persons from other cultures and organisations, approach to time perception, and be able to integrate possible differences of communication styles due to cultural differences. Understanding others – be it through sharing their emotions or reflecting on their thoughts – is a key component of successful social interaction (Kanske et al., 2015).

"Cultural empathy" was coined by Ridley and Lingle (1996, cited in Wang et al., 2003). Cultural empathy extends beyond general empathy to include understanding and accepting another's culture. By employing these insights, Ridley and Lingle provide therapists with the necessary knowledge to work successfully with clients from ethnic backgrounds that are different from their own.

In their view, cultural empathy "requires the deepening of the human empathic response to permit mutuality and understanding across the wide range of differences in value and expectation that cross-cultural exchange often entails" (Ridley & Lingle, p. 22, cited in cited in Vaughn & Johnson, 2021).

According to Wang et al. (2003), cultural and ethnic aspects of empathy are essential. Based on general and cultural empathy theories, they formulated the concept of ethnocultural empathy and tried to operationalize it. According to Wang et al., ethnocultural empathy differs from general empathy in several ways.

The first aspect is to take into consideration the other person's culture. Cultural contexts should not be viewed as separate from the other person, but rather as contexts that interpret and place the experience of the other person. So, in classroom context, when the teacher responds to students' needs, they feel valued, more capable of learning, and more engaged with the learning environment and materials.

The second aspect that distinguishes ethnocultural empathy is the control of one's own subjective per-ception in the form of prejudices against people and groups of different cultures and ethnicities. Qualitative studies have revealed that children use concrete elements and context-dependent strategies to construct and appropriate national identities by drawing upon experiences and narratives with which they are already familiar.

It has been found that the importance of national identity increases with age and that students' understandings of national identity change with age as well, progressing from concrete to abstract elements, always infused with context. Also, it has been noted that children's notions of national identity are often heavily influenced by ethnic markers.

Yet, children demonstrate interest, tolerance, and openness toward dual (national), global, and civil conceptualizations of national identity. Further, children actively construct national identities and appropriate dominant ideas of what it means to belong to and identify with a national group.

Finally, ethnocultural empathic ability combines theory and practical experience, in addition to theoretical knowledge. If one has not encountered individuals from other cultures, or perhaps has not lived for an extended period in another country or has never been in similar situations as these ethnic groups, it is difficult to comprehend other ethnic perspectives.

Previous Research on Ethnocultural Empathy

Empathy for people from other cultures is facilitated by identifying the core components of ethnocultural empathy and factors that facilitate it (Anderson and

Shannon, 1988a). Researchers who acknowledge the importance of cultural and ethnic components have developed a concept called ethnocultural empathy (Wang et al., 2003; Rasoal et al., 2011). Cultural competence, culture empathy, and trans-cultural empathy are also terms associated with this ability (Vaughn and Johnson, 2021).

Besides, according to Wang et al. (2003), ethnocultural empathy is the ability to understand and appreciate the feelings of those from cultures other than the one's own. It is noted that the empathic feeling and expression factor relates to one's own emotional responses to the emotions or experiences of others. To take an empathic perspective, one must understand the ethnic perspective of others (Wang et al., 2003). Culture acceptance involves understanding and accepting elements of different cultures, while empathic awareness refers to the awareness of the cultural experiences of others (Vaughn and Johnson, 2021)

Previous studies have demonstrated that individuals with lower empathy levels are more likely to engage in intergroup aggression, while those with higher empathy levels are more likely to engage in prosocial (Wang et al., 2003) and altruistic behaviours (Ridley & Lingle, 1996, cited in Vaughn and Johnson, 2011).

Understanding other people's cultural characteristics and attributes is essential to cultural empathetic understanding (Vaughn and Johnson, 2021). Ridley and Lingle (1996) argued that feelings, thoughts, and attitudes constitute a person's unique self-experience. Individuals are cultural beings because their self-experiences are inherent in the context of the cultures that shaped them (Ridley & Lingle, 1996).

Culturally empathetic individuals must be able to communicate what they understand about another individual's concerns (Ridley & Lingle, 1996). It must have been communicated in a way that supported the other individual's perception of being understood (Ridley & Lingle, 1996).

Ethnocultural empathy has four components, according to Wang et al.,

> » Understanding how individuals from different ethnicities think and feel is needed for intellectual empathy (Empathic Perspective Taking, EPT).
> » The principle of communicative empathy focuses on the verbal expression of empathy toward members of other ethnic groups. Empathic Feelings and Expressions (EFE) can also be expressed through actions.
> » Empathic awareness is being aware of how society, the media, and the job market treat other ethnic groups (Ethnocultural Empathy Consciousness, EE).

» The acceptance of cultural differences refers to understanding why other ethnic groups behave as they do, such as wearing traditional clothing or speaking their own language (Anderson and Shannon, 1988).

Again, in multicultural classroom context the multicultural attitudes and perspective taking abilities of teachers are crucial to navigating the complexity of diversity in the classroom. Teachers who possess these qualities can better align their teaching with the needs of their students. In addition, these qualities are malleable, allowing teachers to build on their knowledge of students' values, beliefs, communities, personal lives, and experiences to improve these qualities accept their differences and the needs of their students.

Teaching and Disciplining with Empathy

Empathy is an essential quality for teachers in multicultural classrooms (Dolby, 2012). A productive learning environment is dependent on teacher quality, a positive learning climate, and powerful instruction. Positive learning climates involve the teachers and students working together as a team to help everyone succeed. Empathic awareness is enhanced by experiences that are motivated by motivation (Grant and Hill, 2020).

Teachers can fulfill their professional roles more effectively if they have empathy. Teachers' empathy is often cited as a very important competency, as it facilitates effective communication between the participants in the educational process (Dolby, 2012; Stojiljkovi, Djigi, and Zlatković, 2012). A study found that empathy can enhance classroom teachers' ability to act or respond to adolescents in ways that demonstrate CRP (Warren, 2018).

Although Teachers in multicultural and urban classrooms are believed to be more effective when they demonstrate empathy, still few models exist in this area that can train and prepare teachers to develop empathy as a professional disposition (Banks 2007; Banks and Banks 2010 cite in Warren,2014). Teachers' ability to demonstrate empathy helps them fulfill their professional role successfully (Stojiljkovi, Djigi, and Zlatković, 2012).

Teachers Need to Act Interculturally Empathetically

Intercultural empathy is the skill not only to understand the world as it is understood by a culture different from the individual's own culture but to act increasingly reflexively, affectively, empathetically (Barakos, 2019). Compared to the more familiar concept of "reflection", reflexivity is different. Reflexivity relates to both the social and psychological nature of decision making.

Archer contends that humans make their way through the world by identifying personal concerns upon which to act, yet these concerns are always influenced by, and have an influence on, social and cultural concerns. For Archer (2012, as cited in Lunn Brownlee et al., 2019), reflexivity is characterised as an internal conversation that includes discernment (reflecting on a key issue or aim), deliberation (reflexively weighing up personal and contextual concerns) and dedication (resolved action) (Lunn Brownlee et al., 2019).

A teachers' professional identity is formed by a retrospective view of self-worth, examination of motivation at work, and perception of their role as teachers while thinking about the professional future and continued professional development.

To understand the meaning of the professional identity of teachers, one must recognise and understand the educational context in which they operate and the factors that have influenced them over the years. Teachers who have consolidated their professional identity are aware of the process they undergo, know how to control the process and how they should proceed. Expecting learners to understand an experience they have not had is rather unrealistic. Instead, it seems more feasible to foster understanding of the subjective cultural lens through which experiences are interpreted.

To grasp how situations or issues affect individuals in their day-to-day lives and what reactions or feelings they may engender and why engages a certain degree of imagination. Numerous studies indicate, empathic concern is desirable because it increases the likelihood of having altruistic motivation; that is, of being motivated to increase the feeling of satisfaction of the person being felt with empathy towards him/her.

References

Aboud, F. E. et al. (2012) 'Interventions to reduce prejudice and enhance inclusion and respect for ethnic differences in early childhood: A systematic review', *Developmental Review*, 32(4), pp. 307-336. doi: 10.1016/j.dr.2012.05.001.

Alderson, P. (2018) 'How the rights of all school students and teachers are affected by special educational needs or disability (SEND) services: Teaching, psychology, policy', *London Review of Education*, 16(2), pp. 175-190. doi: 10.18546/LRE.16.2.01.

Alphen, P 2011, 'Imagination as a transformative tool in primary school education', vol. 2, no.2, pp. 16-34

Alford, J. H. (2014) 'Alford 2014', 13(3), pp. 71-88.

American, N. (2022) 'Competence and Racial Awareness in Classroom', (2010), pp. 111-128.

Albiero, P. and Matricardi, G. (2013) 'Empathy towards people of different race and ethnicity: Further empirical evidence for the Scale of Ethnocultural Empathy', *International Journal of Intercultural Relations*, 37(5), pp. 648-655. doi: 10.1016/j.ijintrel.2013.05.003.

Anderson, E. M. and Shannon, A. L. (1988) 'Toward a Conceptualization of Mentoring', *Journal of Teacher Education*, 39(1), pp. 38-42. doi: 10.1177/002248718803900109.

Anderson, J. R. 1983. *The architecture of cognition*. Cambridge, MA: Harvard University Press.

References

ARASARATNAM, L. A. (2007) 'Research in intercultural communication competence', *Journal of International Communication*, 13(2), pp. 66–73. doi: 10.1080/13216597.2007.9674715.

Arasaratnam, L., Banerjee, S. and Dembek, K. (2010) 'The integrated model of intercultural communication competence (IMICC)', *Australian Journal of Communication*, 37(3), p. 103.

Arasaratnam, L. A. (2014) 'A discussion of multiculturalism in Australia from educators' perspective', SpringerPlus, 3(1), pp. 1–8. doi: 10.1186/2193-1801-3-36.

Arasaratnam, L. A. (2006) 'Further testing of a new model of intercultural communication competence', *Communication Research Reports*, 23(2), pp. 93–99. doi: 10.1080/08824090600668923.

Arasaratnam, L. A. and Doerfel, M. L. (2005) 'Intercultural communication competence: Identifying key components from multicultural perspectives', *International Journal of Intercultural Relations*, 29(2), pp. 137–163. doi: 10.1016/j.ijintrel.2004.04.001.

Arrowsmith, C. and Mandla, V. R. (2017) 'Institutional approaches for building intercultural understanding into the curriculum: an Australian perspective', *Journal of Geography in Higher Education*, 41(4), pp. 475–487. doi: 10.1080/03098265.2017.1337733.

Assing Hvidt, E. *et al.* (2020) 'Development in Danish medical students' empathy: Study protocol of a cross-sectional and longitudinal mixed-methods study', *BMC Medical Education*, 20(1), pp. 1–9. doi: 10.1186/s12909-020-1967-2.

Ausubel, D. P. 1963. *The psychology of meaningful verbal learning*. New York: Grune and Stration.

Barakos, E. (2019) 'Multilingual language trainers as language workers: a discourse-ethnographic investigation', *Language and Intercultural Communication*, 19(2), pp. 184–200. doi: 10.1080/14708477.2018.1487971.

Baron, A. S. and Banaji, M. R. (2006) 'The development of implicit attitudes', *Psychological Science*, 17(1), pp. 53–58. Available at: 10.1111/j.1467-9280.2005.01664.x%5Cn http://search.ebscohost.com/login.aspx?direct=true&db=a9h&AN=19185524&site=ehost-live.

Baron-Cohen, S. and Wheelwright, S. (2004) 'The empathy quotient: An investigation of adults with asperger syndrome or high functioning autism, and normal sex differences', *Journal of Autism and Developmental Disorders*, 34(2), pp. 163–175. doi: 10.1023/B:JADD.0000022607.19833.00.

Barton, K. C. and Ho, L. C. (2020) 'Cultivating sprouts of benevolence: a foundational principle for curriculum in civic and multicultural education', *Multicultural Education Review*, 12(3), pp. 157–176. doi: 10.1080/2005615X.2020.1808928.

Bassey, M. O. (2016) 'Culturally responsive teaching: Implications for educational justice', *Education Sciences*, 6(4). doi: 10.3390/educsci6040035.

Beauchamp, C. and Thomas, L. (2009) 'Understanding teacher identity: An overview of issues in the literature and implications for teacher education', *Cambridge Journal of Education*, 39(2), pp. 175–189. doi: 10.1080/03057640902902252.

Bennett, C.I.1999, *Comprehensive multicultural education*. Boston: Allyn & Bacon.

Bennett, M. (1998) 'Intercultural communication: A current perspective', *Basic concepts of intercultural communication: Selected readings*, (January 1998), pp. 1–20. Available at: http://www.mairstudents.info/6b.Bennett.pdf.

Bennett, M. J 1986, 'A developmental approach to training for intercultural sensitivity', *International Journal of Intercultural Relations,* vol. 10, no. 2, pp. 179-196.

Bevir, M. and Stueber, K. (2011) 'Empathy, rationality, and explanation', *Journal of the Philosophy of History*, 5(2), pp. 147–162. doi: 10.1163/187226311X582293.

Bhopal, K. and Rhamie, J. (2014) 'Initial teacher training: understanding "race," diversity and inclusion', *Race Ethnicity and Education*, 17(3), pp. 304–325. doi: 10.1080/13613324.2013.832920.

Bidwell, C. E and Friedkin, N.E 1988

Biesta, G., Priestley, M. and Robinson, S. (2015) 'The role of beliefs in teacher agency', *Teachers and Teaching: Theory and Practice*, 21(6), pp. 624–640. coi: 10.1080/13540602.2015.1044325.

Bigge, M. L. 1976. *Learning theories for teaches* (3ed.). New York: Harper and Row Publishers

Billiot, T. and Forbes, L. P. (2020) 'Enhancing student empathy through the taxonomy of significant learning', *Journal of International Education in Business*, 14(1), pp. 130–143. doi: 10.1108/JIEB-04-2020-0033.

Blessett, B. (2018) 'Embedding cultural competence and racial justice in public administration programs', *Journal of Public Affairs Education*, 24(4), pp. 425–429. doi: 10.1080/15236803.2018.1520383.

Bond, A. C. (2020) *Indigenous knowledges, Indigenous educators and culturally safe pedagogies Final report 2020.*

Bonner, P. J., Warren, S. R. and Jiang, Y. H. (2018) 'Voices from urban classrooms: Teachers' perceptions on instructing diverse students and using culturally responsive teaching', *Education and Urban Society*, 50(8), pp. 697–726. doi: 10.1177/0013124517713820.

Booysen, L (ed.). 2003, 'Diversity Management. In Slabbert JA, Prinsloo JJ, Swanepool BJ and Backer' W (eds.), *Managing Employment Relations in South Africa*, Butterworth: Lexis Nexis.

Bourdieu, P. and Passeron, J. 1977 *Reproduction in Education, Society and Culture.* London: Sage.

Brayboy, B. M. J., & Maughan, E 2009, 'Indigenous knowledges and the story of the bean'. *Harvard Educational Review*, vol.79, no.1, pp1-21.

Brown, D 2007, *'Principles of Language Learning and Teaching'* (5th Ed), New Jersey: Prentice Hall.

Brown, H. & Cambourne, B 1987, *Read and retell: A strategy for the whole language/natural learning classroom.* Portsmouth, NH: Heinemann.

Bruner, J. S. 1967, *On knowing.* New York: Atheneum.

Burns, R 1995. *The adult learner at work.* Sydney: Business and Professional Publishing.

Butcher, A. 2008, 'Linguistic aspects of Australian Aboriginal English. Clinical Linguistics and Phonetics', vol.22, no.8, pp.625–642. http://informahealthcare.com/doi/abs/10.1080/02699200802223535

Cachia, R., Ferrari, A., Ala-Mutka, K., Punie, Y 2010 *Creative Learning and Innovative Teaching Final Report on the Study on Creativity and Innovation in Education in the EU Member States.*

Carlo, A. *et al.* (2013) 'Study on Policy Measures to Improve the Attractiveness of the Teaching Profession in Europe. Final Report (contract n° EAC-2010-1391)', *March*, 1(December), p. 79.

Carter, E. W. (2018) 'Supporting the Social Lives of Secondary Students With Severe Disabilities: Considerations for Effective Intervention', *Journal of Emotional and Behavioral Disorders*, 26(1), pp. 52–61. doi: 10.1177/1063426617739253.

Casale, C. and Simmons, T. (2018) 'Developing Empathetic Learners', *Journal of Thought*, 52(3-4), p. 3.

Catarci, M. (2013) 'Interculturalism in Italian primary schools with a high concentration of immigrant students', *Intercultural Education*, 24(5), pp. 456–475. doi: 10.1080/14675986.2013.827946.

Cebrián, G. and Junyent, M. (2015) 'Competencies in education for sustainable development: Exploring the student teachers' views', *Sustainability (Switzerland)*, 7(3), pp. 2768–2786. doi: 10.3390/su7032768.

Chen, C. (2013) 'Empathy in language learning and its inspiration to the development of intercultural communicative competence', *Theory and Practice in Language Studies*, 3(12), pp. 2267–2273. doi: 10.4304/tpls.3.12.2267-2273.

Chen, D. and Yang, X. (2017) 'Improving Active Classroom Participation of ESL Students: Applying Culturally Responsive Teaching Strategies', *Theory and Practice in Language Studies*, 7(1), p. 79. doi: 10.17507/tpls.0701.10.

Chenowith (2014) 'Reproduced with permission of the copyright owner . Further reproduction prohibited without', *Journal of Allergy and Clinical Immunology*, 44(1), pp. 35–40. Available at: http://dx.doi.org/10.1016/j.jaci.2012.05.050.

Cho, G. & DeCastro-Ambrosetti, D 2006, 'Insight into Teachers' View of Minority Parents' Attitudes toward Education: Who cares?', Paper presented at the annual conference of the American Educational Research Association (AERA), San Francisco, California.

References

Christov-Moore, L. *et al.* (2016) *Empathy: Gender effects in brain and behaviour, Neuroscience and Biobehavioral Reviews*. doi: 10.1016/j.neubiorev.2014.09.001.Empathy.

Collier, V. P. (1987) 'Academic Purposes', 21(4).

Collier, V. P. and Thomas, W. P. (2014) 'Creating Dual Language Schools For A Transformed World: Administrators Speak', pp. 1–13.

Collins, C. S. and Rhoads, R. A. (2008) 'The World Bank and higher education in the developing world: The cases of Uganda and Thailand', *International Perspectives on Education and Society*, 9(08), pp. 177–221. doi: 10.1016/S1479-3679(08)00007-8.

Collucci, M. A. (2022) 'teacher preparation for linguistically rich classrooms: a Qualitative case stuDy of take-up in relation to linguistically responsive teaching', *Journal of Ethnographic & Qualitative Research*, 16, pp. 207–2027.

Coskun, K. (2019) 'Development of facial emotion recognition and empathy test (FERET) for primary school children', *Children Australia*, 44(1), pp. 23–31. doi: 10.1017/cha.2018.51.

Creswell, J., & Creswell, D. (2018). Research design: Qualitative, quanti- tative, and mixed methods approaches (5th ed.). SAGE Publication.

Cross, J. R. *et al.* (2018) 'A Comparison of Perceptions of Barriers to Academic Success Among High-Ability Students From High- and Low-Income Groups Exposing

Cross, T.L., Bazron, B.I., Dennis, K. W., & Issacs, M.R 1989. *Toward a culturally competent system of care: vol. 1. A monograph on effective services for minority children who are severely emotionally disturbed.* Washington, DC: Poverty of a Different Kind', *Gifted Child Quarterly*, 62(1), pp. 111–129. doi: 10.1177/0016986217738050.

Dandy, J. and Pe-Pua, R. (2010) 'Attitudes to multiculturalism, immigration and cultural diversity: Comparison of dominant and non-dominant groups in three Australian states', *International Journal of Intercultural Relations*, 34(1), pp. 34–46. doi: 10.1016/j.ijintrel.2009.10.003.

Dandy, J. et al. (2015) 'Academic Expectations of Australian Students from Aboriginal, Asian and Anglo Backgrounds: Perspectives of Teachers, Trainee-teachers and Students', *International Journal of Disability, Development and Education*, 62(1), pp. 60–82. doi: 10.1080/1034912X.2014.984591.

Dare, L. and Nowicki, E. (2018) 'Strategies for inclusion: Learning from students' perspectives on acceleration in inclusive education', *Teaching and Teacher Education*, 69, pp. 243–252. doi: 10.1016/j.tate.2017.10.017.

Darling, Hammoud Burns, D., Campbell, C., Goodwin, A. L., Hammerness, K., Low, E., ... Zeichner, K. (2017) *What Kinds of Policies Affect Teaching?*

Davis, M. H. (1983). Measuring individual differences in empathy: Evidence for a multidimensional approach. *Journal of Personality and Social Psychology, 44*(1), 113–126. https://doi.org/10.1037/0022-3514.44.1.113

Davis, M. H., Luce, C. and Kraus, S. J. (1994) 'The Heritability of Characteristics Associated with Dispositional Empathy', *Journal of Personality*, 62(3), pp. 369–391. doi: 10.1111/j.1467-6494.1994.tb00302.x.

Deardorff, D. K. (2004). The identification and assessment of intercultural competence as a student outcome of internationalization at in situations of higher education in the United States.), (Doctoral dissertation). Retrieved from the North Carolina State University Library. (http://www.lib.ncsu.edu/resolver/1840.16/5733) North Carolina State University, Raleigh, NC.

Deardorff, D. K. (2006) 'Identification and assessment of intercultural competence as a student outcome of internationalization', *Journal of Studies in International Education*, 10(3), pp. 241–266. doi: 10.1177/1028315306287002.

Deardorff, D. K., Arasaratnam, L. A., & Calloway-Thomas, C. (2017). The role of empathy in fostering intercultural com- petence. In D. K. Deardorff & L. A. Arasaratnam (Eds.), Intercultural competence in higher education (pp. 32–42). Routledge. (read online could not cite; book chapters)

Decapua, A. (2016) 'Reaching Students with Limited or Interrupted Formal Education Through Culturally Responsive Teaching', *Language and Linguistics Compass*, 10(5), pp. 225–237. doi: 10.1111/lnc3.12183.

DeCapua, A. and Marshall, H. W. (2015) 'Reframing the Conversation About Students With Limited or Interrupted Formal Education: From Achievement Gap to Cultural Dissonance', *NASSP Bulletin*, 99(4), pp. 356–370. doi: 10.1177/0192636515620662.

Denzin, N., & Lincoln, Y. (2011). The SAGE handbook of qualitative research (4th ed.). SAGE Publications.

DiMaggio, P 1982 'Cultural Capital and School Success: The Impact of Status Culture Participation on the Grades of US High School Students' American Sociological Review vol.47, no.2, pp.189-201

Dimitrova-gyuzeleva, S. (2019) 'Developing int e rcultural communicative comp e tence – the two sides of the coin', 2019(2), pp. 15–25.

Diversity Training University International DTUI 2011 <http://www.dtui.com/qapg1.html>

Dolby, N. (2012) 'Rethinking multicultural education for the next generation: The new empathy and social justice', *Rethinking Multicultural Education For The Next Generation: The New Empathy and Social Justice*, (January), pp. 1–158. doi: 10.4324/9780203124512.

Donahue-Keegan, D., Villegas-Reimers, E. and Cressey, J. (2019) 'Integrating Social-Emotional Learning and Culturally Responsive Teaching in Teacher Education Preparation Programs: The Massachusetts Experience So Far', *Teacher Education Quarterly*, 46(4), p. 150.

Dörnyei, Z. 2001. *Motivational Strateges in the Language Classroom.* Cambridge: Cambridge University Press. http://www.slideshare.net/carlachavezs/motivatonal-strategies-in-the-language-classrocm-dornyei-zoltan

Drewelow, I. and Finney, S. (2020) 'Developing intercultural empathy through a strategy-based simulation in intermediate Spanish', *Language Learning Journal*, 48(6), pp. 754–767. doi: 10.1080/09571736.2018.1448433.

Duncan-Andrade, J.M.R, in Teel.K.M. &Obidah, J.E. (2008). Building racial and cultural competence in the classroom (pp. 111-126) New York: Teachers College Press,

DuPraw, M. E. and Axner, M 1997, *Toward a more perfect union in an age of diversity: Working or common cross-cultural communication challenges*, Topsfield Foundation and Marci Reaven.

Edlins, M. and Dolamore, S. (2018) 'Ready to serve the public? The role of empathy in public service education programs', *Journal of Public Affairs Education*, 24(3), pp. 300–320. doi: 10.1080/15236803.2018.1429824.

Elias, N. M. and D'Agostino, M. J. (2019) 'Gender competency in public administration education', *Teaching Public Administration*, 37(2), pp. 218–233. doi: 10.1177/0144739419840766.

Esser, A. *et al.* (2018) 'A female leadership competency framework from the perspective of male leaders', *Gender in Management*, 33(2), pp. 138–166. doi: 10.1108/GM-06-2017-0077.

Fantini, A. E. (2000) 'A central concern: Developing intercultural competence', *About our institution*, pp. 25–42.

Farmer, T. W. *et al.* (2019) 'Promoting Inclusive Communities in Diverse Classrooms: Teacher Attunement and Social Dynamics Management', *Educational Psychologist*, 54(4), pp. 286–305. doi: 10.1080/00461520.2019.1635020.

Fekete, O. R. *et al.* (2020) 'Salutogenesis as a theoretical framework for psychosocial rehabilitation: the case of the Clubhouse model', *International Journal of Qualitative Studies on Health and Well-being*, 15(1). doi: 10.1080/17482631.2020.1748942.

Fernando, L. and Rodríguez, G. (2013) 'Exploring EFL Pre-Service Teachers' Experience with Cultural Content and Intercultural Communicative Competence at Three Colombian Universities', *Profile: Issues in Teachers´ Professional Development*, 15(2), pp. 49–67.

Figueredo-Canosa, V. *et al.* (2020) 'Teacher Training in Intercultural Education: Teacher Perceptions', *Education Sciences*, 10(3), p. 81. doi: 10.3390/educsci10030081.

Fischer, A. R., Jome, L. M. and Atkinson, D. R. (1998) 'Reconceptualizing Multicultural Counseling: Universal Healing Conditions in a Culturally Specific Context', *The Counseling Psychologist*, 26(4), pp. 525–588. doi: 10.1177/0011000098264001.

Flint, A. S. and Jaggers, W. (2021) 'You matter here: The impact of asset-based pedagogies on learning', *Theory into Practice*, 60(3), pp. 254–264. doi: 10.1080/00405841.2021.1911483.

Forrest, J., Lean, G. and Dunn, K. (2016) 'Challenging racism through schools: teacher attitudes to cultural diversity and multicultural education in Sydney, Australia', *Race Ethnicity and Education*, 19(3), pp. 618–638. doi: 10.1080/13613324.2015.1095170. Gallas, K 2001, 'Look, Karen, I'm running like jell-o: 'Imagination as a question, a topic, a tool for literacy research and learning', Research in the Teaching of English, vol. 35, no. 4, pp. 457-492

G Thompson, I. C. (2019) 'Education policy-making and time', in *G Thompson, I Cook*. doi: 10.1016/0001-4575(80)90044-5.

Gambrell, L. B., & Dromsky, A 2000, Fostering reading comprehension. In D. S. Strickland & L. M. Morrow (Eds.), Beginning reading and writing (pp. 143-153). New York, NY: Teachers College Press.

Gardner, R.C., and Lambert, W.E. (1972). *Attitudes and Motivation in Second Language Learning*. Rowley, MA: Newbury House

Gest, S. D. *et al.* (2014) 'Teacher Management of Elementary Classroom Social Dynamics: Associations With Changes in Student Adjustment', *Journal of Emotional and Behavioral Disorders*, 22(2), pp. 107–118. doi: 10.1177/1063426613512677.

Geva, E., & Olson, D 1983, 'Children's story-retelling'. First Language, vol.4, pp.85-109.

Gibson, A , Gold, J. and Sgouros, C 2003 The Power of Story Retelling *The Tutor*

Gorski, P. C. (2009) 'What we're teaching teachers: An analysis of multicultural teacher education coursework syllabi', *Teaching and Teacher Education*, 25(2), pp. 309–318. doi: 10.1016/j.tate.2008.07.008.

Gottfried (2014) 'the Positive Peer Effects', 115(1).

Grant, C. A. (1994) *Best Practices in Teacher Preparation for Urban Schools: Lessons from the Multicultural Teacher Education Literature, Action in Teacher Education*. doi: 10.1080/01626620.1994.10463204.

Grant, D. E. . and Hill, J. B. (2020) 'Activating Culturally Empathic Motivation in Diverse Students', *Journal of Education and Learning*, 9(5), p. 45. doi: 10.5539/jel.v9n5p45.

Halász, G. (2019) 'Designing and implementing teacher policies using competence frameworks as an integrative policy tool', *European Journal of Education*, pp. 323–336. doi: 10.1111/ejed.12349.

Hammond, J. (2014) 'An Australian perspective on standards-based education, teacher knowledge, and students of english as an additional language', *TESOL Quarterly*, 48(3), pp. 507–532. doi: 10.1002/tesq.173.

Harrison, N. and Clarke, I. (2022) 'Decolonising curriculum practice: developing the indigenous cultural capability of university graduates', *Higher Education*, 83(1), pp. 183–197. doi: 10.1007/s10734-020-00648-6.

Havrilova, L. *et al.* (2021) 'Introduction of Intercultural Communication Studies into the Curriculum of Pedagogical University', *Revista Romaneasca pentru Educatie Multidimensionala*, 13(3), pp. 448–467. doi: 10.18662/rrem/13.3/461.

Henkin, R. & Steinmetz, L 2008, 'The Need for Diversity Education as Perceived by Preservice Teachers', *Journal of the Scholarship of Teaching and Learning*, no. 8, pp. 101-109.

Hofstede, G. J. (2009). The Moral Circle in Intercultural Competence: Trust Across Cultures. In Deardorff, D. K. (ed) The SAGE Handbook of Intercultural Competence. Sage. 85-99.p

Holcomb-McCoy, C 2005, 'Investigating School Counselors' Perceived Multicultural Competence', *Professional School Counseling*, no. 8, pp. 414-423. http://www.pbs.org/ampu/crosscult.html

Holdsworth, S. and Maynes, N. (2017) '"But what if i fail?" A meta-synthetic study of the conditions supporting teacher innovation', *Canadian Journal of Education*, 40(4), pp. 665–703.

Holm, N. (no date) 'JOURNAL OF CHRISTIAN EDUCATION, Vol . 40, No.2 July 1 997 FORGING A COSMOPOLITAN AUSTRALIA: MULTICULTURALISM AND EDUCATION IN THE 'NINETIES NEIL HOLM', (2).

Howard, G. (2006). We can't teach what we don't know: White teachers, multiracial Schools. New York: Teachers College Press.

Huda, M. *et al.* (2017) 'Empowering learning culture as student identity construction in higher education', *Student Culture and Identity in Higher Education*, pp. 160–179. doi: 10.4018/978-1-5225-2551-6.ch010.

Hughes, H. & Hughes, M 2012 *Indigenous education* /Centre for Independent Studies (Australia)

Hugo, G. (2013) 'The changing demographics of Australia over the last 30 years', *Australasian Journal on Ageing*, 32(SUPPL.2), pp. 18–27. doi: 10.1111/ajag.12113.

Ingvarson, L., Beavis, A. and Kleinhenz, E. (2007) 'Factors affecting the impact of teacher education programmes on teacher preparedness: Implications for accreditation policy', *European Journal of Teacher Education*, 30(4), pp. 351–381. doi: 10.1080/02619760701664151.

Isbell, R. T 2002, 'Telling and retelling stories: Learning language and literacy. Young Children, vol.57, pp.26-30. Retrieved from http://www.naeyc.org/yc/.

John-Steiner, V. and Mahn, H. (2003) 'Sociocultural Contexts for Teaching and Learning', *Handbook of Psychology*, (April 2003). doi: 10.1002/0471264385.wei0707.

References

John O. Summers (2001) 'Editorial Staff Book Reviews Marketing and the Law Editorial Review Board', *Journal of the Academy of Marketing Science*, 29(4), pp. 405–4015.

Johnson, J. P., Lenartowicz, T. and Apud, S. (2006) 'Cross-cultural competence in international business: Toward a definition and a model', *Journal of International Business Studies*, 37(4), pp. 525–543. doi: 10.1057/palgrave.jibs.8400205.

Jordan, G. M. and J. (2019) 'The role of empathy in teaching culturally diverse students: a qualitative study of teachers' beliefs', *Teachers and Teaching: Theory and Practice*, 25(5), pp. 507–522. doi: 10.1080/13540602.2019.1602518.

Jung, C. G. 1967, 'The development of personality' 1991 ed. Vol. 17 ISBN 0-691-01838-3. London: Routledge.

Kamp, A. (2018) 'Assembling the actors: exploring the challenges of "system leadership" in education through Actor-Network Theory', *Journal of Education Policy*, 33(6), pp. 778–792. doi: 10.1080/02680939.2017.1380231.

Kamp, A. and Mansouri, F. (2010) 'Constructing inclusive education in a neo-liberal context: Promoting inclusion of Arab-Australian students in an Australian context', *British Educational Research Journal*, 36(5), pp. 733–744. doi: 10.1080/01411920903142958.

Kanske, P. *et al.* (2015) 'Dissecting the social brain: Introducing the EmpaToM to reveal distinct neural networks and brain-behavior relations for empathy and Theory of Mind', *NeuroImage*, 122, pp. 6–19. doi: 10.1016/j.neuroimage.2015.07.082.

Kasl, E. and Yorks, L. (2016) 'Do I Really Know You? Do You Really Know Me? Empathy Amid Diversity in Differing Learning Contexts', *Adult Education Quarterly*, 66(1), pp. 3–20. doi: 10.1177/0741713615606965.

Keahey, H. L. (2021) 'Reflections on empathic design: a K-16 perspective', *Educational Technology Research and Development*, 69(1), pp. 73–76. doi: 10.1007/s11423-020-09895-x.

Kelly-jackson, C. *et al.* (2016) 'Preparing Students to Teach in Diverse Classrooms : Voice of a Former Intern-Now PDS Teacher WAS TO PROVIDE OPPORTUNITIES FOR KSU STUDENTS TO BECOME CHANGE AGENTS IN THEIR COMMUNITIES AND EMPOWERED TO IMPROVE THE ACADEMIC ACHIEVEMENT', pp. 14–16.

Kember, D., & Gow, L. 1994, 'Orientations to Teaching and Their Effect on The Quality of Student Learning'. Journal of Higher Education, vol. 65, no.1

Khairova, I. and Zakirova, V. (2019) 'Development of Future Primary School Teachers' Linguistic and Methodological Competence', *V International Forum on Teacher Education*, 1, pp. 465–473. doi: 10.3897/ap.1.e0314.

King, S 2004, Pre-Service Teachers' Perception and Knowledge of Multicultural Education. Education Specialist Thesis, University of South Florida.

Klees, S. J. (2002) 'World Bank education policy: New rhetoric, old ideology', *International Journal of Educational Development*, 22(5), pp. 451–474. doi: 10.1016/S0738-0593(02)00006-8.

Klees, S. J. et al. (2020) 'The World Bank's SABER: A Critical Analysis', 64(1), pp. 46–66.

Kleinhenz, E. and Ingvarson, L. (2004) 'Teacher accountability in australia: Current policies and practices and their relation to the improvement of teaching and learning', *Research Papers in Education*, 19(1), pp. 31–49. doi: 10.1080/0267152032000176963.

Klenowski, V., & Gertz, T. 2009, Culture-fair assessment leading to culturally responsive pedagogy with Indigenous students. Presented at the ACER Research Conference Perth, Australia.

Kokkinos, C. M. and Kipritsi, E. (2018) 'Bullying, moral disengagement and empathy: exploring the links among early adolescents', *Educational Psychology*, 38(4), pp. 535–552. doi: 10.1080/01443410.2017.1363376.

Kolb, D 1984. *Experiential learning. Experience as a source of learning and development*. Englewood Cliffs, NNJ: Prentice Hall.

Koskinen, P. S., Gambrell, L. B., Kapinus, B. A., & Heathington, B. S 1988, 'Retelling: A strategy for enhancing students' reading comprehension'. *Reading Teacher, vol.41*, pp.892-896. Retrieved from http://onlinelibrary.wiley.com/journal/10.1002/ %28ISSN%291936-2714

Laird S (2013) *Cultural Competence in Social Work*, SAGE Publications Ltd. doi: 10.4135/9781446269473.n3.

Lee, J., Lee, Y. and Kim, M. H. (2018) 'Effects of Empathy-based Learning in Elementary Social Studies', *Asia-Pacific Education Researcher*, 27(6), pp. 509–521. doi: 10.1007/s40299-018-0413-2.

Levin, B 2003 *Approaches to Equity in Policy for Lifelong Learning.* The University of Manitoba, Winnipeg, Canada.

Longobardi, C. et al. (2021) 'Student–teacher relationship quality and prosocial behaviour: The mediating role of academic achievement and a positive attitude towards school', *British Journal of Educational Psychology*, 91(2), pp. 547–562. doi: 10.1111/bjep.12378.

López-Pérez, B. et al. (2017) 'Cognitive and Affective Empathy, Personal Belief in a Just World, and Bullying Among Offenders', *Journal of Interpersonal Violence*, 32(17), pp. 2591–2604. doi: 10.1177/0886260515593300.

Lum, D (Ed.). 2005, *Cultural competence, practice stages, and client systems.* Belmont, CA: Thomson Brooks/Cole.

Lunn Brownlee, J. et al. (2019) 'Researching teacher educators' preparedness to teach to and about diversity: investigating epistemic reflexivity as a new conceptual framework', *Asia-Pacific Journal of Teacher Education*, 47(3), pp. 230–250. doi: 10.1080/1359866X.2018.1555794.

Lutovac, S. and Assunção Flores, M. (2021) '"Those who fail should not be teachers": Pre-service Teachers' Understandings of Failure and Teacher Identity Development', *Journal of Education for Teaching*, 47(3), pp. 379–394. doi: 10.1080/02607476.2021.1891833.
Malin, M., & Maidment, D 2003, 'Education, Indigenous survival and well-being: Emerging ideas and programs'. *The Australian Journal of Indigenous Education, vol.32, pp.*85-99.

Lynch, S. A. and Simpson, C. G. (2010) 'Social Skills: Laying the Foundation for Success', *Dimensions of Early Childhood*, 38(2), pp. 3–12. Available at: https://search.ebscohost.com/login.aspx?direct=true&db=er c&AN=EJ945679&site=ehost-live%5Cnhttp://www.southernearlychildhood.org/publications.php.

Martines, D 2005, 'Teacher Perceptions of Multicultural Issues in School Settings', *The Qualitative Report*, no. 10, pp. 1-20.

Madlinske, michelle attard tonna & J. (2018) *Teacher education policy and practice, Teacher education policy and practice*. doi: 10.47050/9949290239.

Magid, B. and Shane, E. (2017) 'Relational Self Psychology', *Psychoanalysis, Self and Context*, 12(1), pp. 3–19. doi: 10.1080/15551024.2017.1251176.

Mardiana, Siska; Suminar, Jenny Ratna, Sugiana, D. S. (2019) 'University of Nebraska - Lincoln DigitalCommons @ University of Nebraska - Lincoln', 43(12), pp. 2–14.

Markus, A. (2014) 'Attitudes to immigration and cultural diversity in Australia', *Journal of Sociology*, 50(1), pp. 10–22. doi: 10.1177/1440783314522188

Martin, J. & Sugarman, J 1993, *Models of Classroom Management* (2nd ed.). Bellingham, Washington: Temeron Books Inc

Marton, F., Dall'Alba, G., & Beaty, E. 1993. Conceptions of learning. International Journal of Educational Research, 19, 277-300.

Marton, F., Hounsell, D., & Entwistle, N 1997. *The experience of leaning: Implications for teaching and studying in higher education*. Edinburgh: Scottish Academic Press.

Maslow, A. (1970). *Motivation and personality* (2nd ed.). New York: Harper & Row.http://www.slideshare.net/carlachavezs/motivatonal-strategies-in-the-language-classroom-dornyei-zoltan

Maslow, A. (1987). *Motivation and personality.* (3rd ed., revised by R. Frager, J. Fadiman, C. McReynolds, & R. Cox ed.). New York: Harper & Row.http://www.osaka-gu.ac.jp/php/kelly/papers/motivation.html

Maslow, A. H. 1970, *Motivation and personality*. New York: Harper and Row Publishers.

Masto, M. (2015) 'Empathy and its role in morality', *Southern Journal of Philosophy*, 53(1), pp. 74–96. doi: 10.1111/sjp.12097.

Matveev, A. V. and Nelson, P. E. (2004) 'Cross cultural communication competence and multicultural team performance: Perceptions of American and Russian managers', *International Journal of Cross Cultural Management*, 4(2), pp. 253–270. doi: 10.1177/1470595804044752.

McAllister, G. and Irvine, J. J. (2002) 'The Role of Empathy in Teaching Culturally Diverse Students', *Journal of Teacher Education*, pp. 433–443. doi: 10.1177/002248702237397.

Mendenhall, M. *et al.* (2021) 'Teachers as agents of change: positive discipline for inclusive classrooms in Kakuma refugee camp', *International Journal of Inclusive Education*, 25(2), pp. 147–165. doi: 10.1080/13603116.2019.1707300.

Meng, C. *et al.* (2021) 'Processing of expressions by individuals with autistic traits : Empathy deficit or sensory', pp. 1–18.

Mensah, F. M. (2021) 'CulturallyRelevant and Culturally Responsive: Two Theories of Practice for Science Teaching', *National Science Teaching Associatiom*, 58(4), pp. 2009–2012.

Miklikowska, M. (2018) 'Empathy trumps prejudice: The longitudinal relation between empathy and anti-immigrant attitudes in adolescence', *Developmental Psychology*, 54(4), pp. 703–717. doi: 10.1037/dev0000474.

Miles, M. B., Huberman, A.M 1994, Qualitative data analysis: An expanded sourcebook (2nd ed.). Londan: Sage

Miller, R.K 2009, *On Becoming an Important and Constant Contributor: Deepening Our Culture of Innovation*.

Milner IV, R. R. (2011) 'Culturally Relevant Pedagogy in a Diverse Urban Classroom', *Urban Review*, 43(1), pp. 66–89. doi: 10.1007/s11256-009-0143-0.

Min, M. *et al.* (2022) 'What Empowers Teachers to Become Social Justice-Oriented Change Agents? Influential Factors on Teacher Agency toward Culturally Responsive Teaching', *Education and Urban Society*, 54(5), pp. 560–584. doi: 10.1177/00131245211027511.

Mockler, N. (2013) 'Teacher professional learning in a neoliberal age: Audit, professionalism and identity', *Australian Journal of Teacher Education*, 38(10), pp. 35–47. doi: 10.14221/ajte.2013v38n10.8.

Moje, E. B. (2007) 'Developing socially just subject-matter instruction: A review of the literature on disciplinary literacy teaching', *Review of Research in Education*, 31(March), pp. 1–44. doi: 10.3102/0091732X07300046.

Morrow, L 1996, *Motivating Reading and Writing in Diverse Classrooms.* Social and Physical Contexts in a Literature-Based Program Rutgers University.

Nadeem (2018) '아베 정권의 외교 · 안보 정책과 대북 정책 : 제 1 · 2 · 3 차 내각을 중심으로', 일본연구논총, 06(48), pp. 65–86. doi: 10.24312/paradigms120202.

Nadeem, M. U. (2022) 'An Extension of the Integrated Model of Intercultural Communication Competence (IMICC) with Religiosity: An International Students' Perspective', *SAGE Open*, 12(1). doi: 10.1177/21582440221082139.

Nadeem, M. U., Mohammed, R. and Dalib, S. (2020) 'Retesting integrated model of intercultural communication competence (IMICC) on international students from the Asian context of Malaysia', *International Journal of Intercultural Relations*, 74(September 2019), pp. 17–29. doi: 10.1016/j.ijintrel.2019.10.005.

Nechifor, A. and Borca, A. (2020) 'Contextualising Culture in Teaching a Foreign Language: the Cultural Element among Cultural Awareness, Cultural Competency and Cultural Literacy', *Philologica Jassyensia*, 16(2), pp. 287–304.

Nguyen, T. N. M. *et al.* (2022) 'The use of theory in qualitative research: Challenges, development of a framework and exemplar', *Journal of Advanced Nursing*, 78(1), pp. e21–e28. doi: 10.1111/jan.15053.

Nielsen, B. L. *et al.* (2019) 'Social, emotional and intercultural competencies: a literature review with a particular focus on the school staff', *European Journal of Teacher Education*, 42(3), pp. 410–428. doi: 10.1080/02619768.2019.1604670.

Norris, S. P. and Phillips, L. M. (2003) 'How Literacy in Its Fundamental Sense Is Central to Scientific Literacy', *Science Education*, 87(2), pp. 224–240. doi: 10.1002/sce.10066.

Novikova, I. A. *et al.* (2022) 'Cognitive Abilities and Academic Achievement as Intercultural Competence Predictors in Russian School Students', *Journal of Intelligence*, 10(2). doi: 10.3390/jintelligence10020025.

Ollerhead, S. (2020) '"The pre-service teacher tango": pairing literacy and science in multilingual Australian classrooms', *International Journal of Science Education*, 42(14), pp. 2493–2512. doi: 10.1080/09500693.2019.1634852.

Osborne, J. (2007) *Engaging young people with science: Thoughts about future direction of science education, Promoting scientific literacy: Science education research in transaction*. Available at: http://dx.doi.org/10.1016/j.sbspro.2012.06.510.

Overgaauw, S. *et al.* (2014) 'Behavior and neural correlates of empathy in adolescents', *Developmental Neuroscience*, 36(3–4), pp. 210–219. doi: 10.1159/000363318.

Owocki, G 1999, *Literacy through play*. Portsmouth, NH: Heinemann.

Park, S., Choi, A. and Reynolds, W. M. (2020) 'Cross-national investigation of teachers' pedagogical content knowledge (PCK) in the U.S. and South Korea: what proxy measures of teacher quality are related to PCK?', *International Journal of Science Education*, 42(15), pp. 2630–2651. doi: 10.1080/09500693.2020.1823046.

Partington, G. 2003, 'Why Indigenous issues are an essential component of teacher education programs'. *Australian Journal of Teacher Education*, vol.*27.no.2*, pp.39-48.

Peck, N. F., Maude, S. P. and Brotherson, M. J. (2015) 'Understanding Preschool Teachers' Perspectives on Empathy: A Qualitative Inquiry', *Early Childhood Education Journal*, 43(3), pp. 169–179. doi: 10.1007/s10643-014-0648-3.

Perry, L. B. and Southwell, L. (2011) 'Developing intercultural understanding and skills: models and approaches', *Intercultural Education*, 22(6), pp. 453–466. doi: 10.1080/14675986.2011.644948.

Perso, T. F. and Menzies School of Health Research. (2012) *Cultural responsiveness and school education with particular focus on Australia's first peoples : a review & synthesis of the literature.*

Piaget, J. 1936, *the origins of intelligence in children*. New York: International Universities Press

Pionke, J. J. and Graham, R. (2021) 'A Multidisciplinary Scoping Review of Literature Focused on Compassion, Empathy, Emotional Intelligence, or Mindfulness Behaviors and Working with the Public A Multidisciplinary Scoping Review of Literature Focused on Compassion, Empathy, Emotional I', *Journal of Library Administration*, 61(2), pp. 147–184. doi: 10.1080/01930826.2020.1853469.

Poehlmann-Tynan, J. *et al.* (2016) 'A Pilot Study of Contemplative Practices with Economically Disadvantaged Preschoolers: Children's Empathic and Self-Regulatory Behaviors', *Mindfulness*, 7(1), pp. 46–58. doi: 10.1007/s12671-015-0426-3.

Ponterotto, J. G. *et al.* (1994) 'Assessing Multicultural Counseling Competence: A Review of Instrumentation', *Journal of Counseling & Development*, 72(3), pp. 316–322. doi: 10.1002/j.1556-6676.1994.tb00941.x.

Powell, R., Cantrell, S. C. and Rightmyer, E. (2013) 'Teaching and Reaching All Students: An Instructional Model for Closing the Gap: The Culturally Responsive Instruction Observation Protocol Helps Teachers Work Effectively with Diverse Middle Grades Learners and Their Families', *Middle School Journal*, 44(5), pp. 22–30. doi: 10.1080/00940771.2013.11461869.

Pusch, M.D. 2004. Intercultural training in historical perspective. In Handbook of intercul- tural training, 3rd ed. D. Landis, J.M. Bennett, and M.J. Bennett, 13–36. Thousand Oaks, CA: Sage.

Quinn, F. M 1995, *The Principles and practice of nurse education* (3ed.). London: Chapman and Hall.

Ramsden, P. 1992, *Learning to Teach in Higher Education*. London: Routledge.

Ramsden, P. 1995, 'Student Learning Research: Retrospect and Prospect. Higher Education Research and Development', Vol.4, no.1, pp. 51-69.

Rasoal, C. et al. (2011) 'Ethnocultural versus Basic Empathy: Same or Different?', *Psychology*, 02(09), pp. 925–930. doi: 10.4236/psych.2011.29139.

Ratka, A. (2018) 'Empathy and the development of affective skills', *American Journal of Pharmaceutical Education*, 82(10), pp. 1140–1143. doi: 10.5688/ajpe7192.

Redmond, M. V. (1989) 'human relations', *Human Relations*, 42(7), 593.

Rica, C. and Rica, C. (2018) 'The Empathetic EFL Classroom: a Path to Creative Thinking', pp. 161–174.

Rich, E. and Evans, J. (2009) 'Now i am NObody, see me for who i am: The paradox of performativity', *Gender and Education*, 21(1), pp. 1–16. doi: 10.1080/09540250802213131.

Rich, J. V. (2019) 'Do Professions Represent Competence for Entry-to-Practice in Similar Ways? An Exploration of Competence Frameworks through Document Analysis', *International Journal for the Scholarship of Teaching and Learning*, 13(3), pp. 1–9. doi: 10.20429/ijsotl.2019.130305.

Ridley, C. R., Baker, D. M. and Hill, C. L. (2001) 'Critical issues concerning cultural competence', *The Counseling Psychologist*, 29(6), pp. 822–832. doi: 10.1177/0011000001296003.

Roberts, P., Downes, N. and Reid, J. (2022) 'Teacher Education for a Rural-Ready Teaching Force : Swings , Roundabouts , and Slippery Slides ? Teacher Education for a Rural-Ready Teaching Force : Swings , Roundabouts , and Slippery Slides ?', 47(3).

Roberts, W. (2017) 'Trust, empathy and time: Relationship building with families experiencing vulnerability and disadvantage in early childhood education and care services', *Australasian Journal of Early Childhood*, 42(4), pp. 4–12. doi: 10.23965/AJEC.42.4.01.

Robinson, K 2006, *How schools kill creativity*, Retrieved June 15, 2010, from http://www.ted.com/talks/ken_robinson_says_schools_kill_creativity.html.

Robinson.G, Eickelkapm. U, Goodnow.J, Katz. I 2008, *Contexts of Child Development.* Darwin, N. T. : Charles Darwin University.

Rodriguez, L. M. *et al.* (2021) 'Empathy as a predictor of prosocial behavior and the perceived seriousness of delinquent acts: a cross-cultural comparison of Argentina and Spain', *Ethics and Behavior*, 31(2), pp. 91–101. doi: 10.1080/10508422.2019.1705159.

Rogers, C 1969, *Freedom to learn.* Columbus: Merrill

Roiha, A. and Sommier, M. (2021) 'Exploring teachers' perceptions and practices of intercultural education in an international school', *Intercultural Education*, 32(4), pp. 446–463. doi: 10.1080/14675986.2021.1893986.

Romijn, B. R., Slot, P. L. and Leseman, P. P. M. (2021) 'Increasing teachers' intercultural competences in teacher preparation programs and through professional development: A review', *Teaching and Teacher Education*, 98, p. 103236. doi: 10.1016/j.tate.2020.103236.

Roppola, T., &Whitington, V 2014, 'Pedagogies that engage five to eight year old children's imagination and creativity at school'. *Journal of Educational Enquiry* vol. 13, no. 1, pp. 67-81. University of South Australia.

Rosen, B. and Rutigliano, T. (2014) 'The Power of Empathy in the Workplace', *MWorld*, 13(2), pp. 40–43. Available at: http://blogs.hbr.org/2014/04/the-power-of-dignity-in-the-workplace/.

Rowan, L. *et al.* (2021) *How Does Initial Teacher Education Research Frame the Challenge of Preparing Future Teachers for Student Diversity in Schools? A Systematic Review of Literature*, *Review of Educational Research*. doi: 10.3102/0034654320979171.

Rutland, A. and Killen, M. (2015) 'A developmental science approach to reducing prejudice and social exclusion: Intergroup processes, social-cognitive development, and moral reasoning', *Social Issues and Policy Review*, 9(1), pp. 121–154. doi: 10.1111/sipr.12012.

Ryan, S & Hornbeck, A 2007, 'Pedagogy', in RS New & M Cochran (eds.), *Early childhood education [four volumes]: an international encyclopedia,* Praeger Publishers, Westport, CT, pp. 596-598

Salton, Y., Riddle, S. and Baguley, M. (2022) 'The "good" teacher in an era of professional standards: policy frameworks and lived realities', *Teachers and Teaching: Theory and Practice*, 28(1), pp. 51–63. doi: 10.1080/13540602.2021.2017274.

Samuels, A. J. (2018) 'Exploring Culturally Responsive Pedagogy: Teachers' Perspectives on Fostering Equitable and Inclusive Classrooms', *SRATE Journal*, 27(1), pp. 22–30. Available at: https://files.eric.ed.gov/fulltext/EJ1166706.pdf.

Sandra, D. et al. (2016) 'No 主観的健康感を中心とした在宅高齢者における 健康関連指標に関する共分散構造分析Title', Revista CENIC. Ciencias Biológicas, 152(3), p. 28. Available at: http://www.revistaalad.com/pdfs/Guias_ALAD_11_Nov_2013.pdf%0A http://dx.doi.org/10.15446/revfacmed.v66n3.60060.%0A http://www.cenetec.

Santoro, N., Reid, J., Crawford, L 2011, 'Teaching Indigenous Children: Listening To And Learning From Indigenous Teachers'. Journal of Teacher Education. . Vol.36, no.5 p.68.

Schalk-Soekar, S. R. G., van de Vijver, F. J. R. and Hoogsteder, M. (2004) 'Attitudes toward multiculturalism of immigrants and majority members in the Netherlands', *International Journal of Intercultural Relations*, 28(6), pp. 533–550. doi: 10.1016/j.ijintrel.2005.01.009.

Schelfhout, S. *et al.* (2022) 'Intercultural Competence Predicts Intercultural Effectiveness: Test of an Integrative Framework', *International Journal of Environmental Research and Public Health*, 19(8), pp. 1–21. doi: 10.3390/ijerph19084490.

Schmidt, R., Boraie, D. & Kassabgy, O. (1996). Foreign language motivation internal structure and external connections. In R. L. Oxford (Ed.). *Language learning motivation: Pathways to the new century* (pp. 9-70). Honolulu: University of Hawai'i, Second Language Teaching & Curriculum Center. http://nflrc.hawaii.edu/PDFs/SCHMIDT%20Foreign%20language%20motivation.pdf.

Schwarzenthal, M. et al. (2020) 'Reaping the benefits of cultural diversity: Classroom cultural diversity climate and students' intercultural competence', *European Journal of Social Psychology*, 50(2), pp. 323–346. doi: 10.1002/ejsp.2617.

Shantanam, S. and MUELLER (2018) '乳鼠心肌提取 HHS Public Access', Physiology & behavior, 176(1), pp. 139–148. doi: 10.1016/j.jsat.2019.07.009.Drivers.

Shin & Ryan (2017) 'Friend Influence on Early Adolescent Disruptive Behavior : Teacher Emotional Support Matters Friend Influence on Early Adolescent Disruptive Behavior in', 53(November), pp. 114–125.

Skinner, B. F 1989, *The origins of cognitive thought*. Princeton, North Carolina: Merrill Publishing Company .

Skourdoumbis, A. (2013) 'Classroom teacher effectiveness research and inquiry, and its relevance to the development of public education policy: an Australian context', *International Journal of Qualitative Studies in Education*, 26(8), pp. 967–985. doi: 10.1080/09518398.2012.724465.

Skourdoumbis, A. (2014) 'New directions in education? A critique of contemporary policy reforms', *Asia Pacific Journal of Education*, 36(4), pp. 505–517. doi: 10.1080/02188791.2014.961896.

Sleeter, C. E., & Grant, C. A 1994, *Making choices for multicultural education: Five approaches to race, class, & gender*, (2nd ed). New York: Macmillan.

Sleeter, C 2008, Learning to become a racially and culturally competent ally. In J.E. Obadiah & K.M. Teel. Building racial and cultural competence in the classroom (pp,136-151)

Smith, E. and Yasukawa, K. (2017) 'What makes a good VET teacher? Views of Australian VET teachers and students', *International Journal of Training Research*, 15(1), pp. 23–40. doi: 10.1080/14480220.2017.1355301.

Solhaug, T. and Osler, A. (2018) 'Intercultural empathy among Norwegian students: an inclusive citizenship perspective', *International Journal of Inclusive Education*, 22(1), pp. 89–110. doi: 10.1080/13603116.2017.1357768.

Soundy, C. S 1993, 'Let the story begin! Open the box and set out the props'. Childhood Education, vol.69, pp.146-149. Retrieved from http://www.acei.org/childhood-education.

Southcott, J. E. and Joseph, D. (2010) 'Many layers of meaning: Multicultural music education in Victoria, Australia', *International Journal of the Humanities*, 8(2), pp. 189–200. doi: 10.18848/1447-9508/cgp/v08i02/42850.

Spector, J. M. (2015) 'Pedagogical Knowledge', *The SAGE Encyclopedia of Educational Technology*, pp. 44–52. doi: 10.4135/9781483346397.n237.

Spreng, R. N. *et al.* (2009) 'The Toronto empathy questionnaire: Scale development and initial validation of a factor-analytic solution to multiple empathy measures', *Journal of Personality Assessment*, 91(1), pp. 62–71. doi: 10.1080/00223890802484381.

Stojiljković, S., Djigić, G. and Zlatković, B. (2012) 'Empathy and Teachers' Roles', *Procedia - Social and Behavioral Sciences*, 69(Iceepsy), pp. 960–966. doi: 10.1016/j.sbspro.2012.12.021.

Stueber, K. R. (2011) 'Imagination, empathy, and moral deliberation: The case of imaginative resistance', *Southern Journal of Philosophy*, 49(SUPPL. 1), pp. 156–180. doi: 10.1111/j.2041-6962.2011.00065.x.

Sue, D. W. (2001) 'Multidimensional Facets of Cultural Competence', *The Counseling Psychologist*, 29(6), pp. 790–821. doi: 10.1177/0011000001296002.

Sue, D.W. & Sue, D 1990, *Counselling the culturally different: Theory and practice* (2nd ed.). New York: Wiley.

Sue, D.W., Bernier, J.B., Durran, M., Feinberg, L., Pedersen, P., Smith, E., et al. 1982, 'Cross-cultural counseling competencies', *The Counseling Psychologist*, no. 10, pp. 45-52.

Sue, S. (1998) 'In Search of Cultural Competence in Psychotherapy and CounselingSue, S. (1998). In Search of Cultural Competence in Psychotherapy and Counseling. American Psychologist, 53(4), 440–448. https://doi.org/10.1037/0003-066X.53.4.440', *American Psychologist*, 53(4), pp. 440–448.

Syse, H. (2020) 'In Times of Crisis', *Journal of Military Ethics*, 19(1), p. 1. doi: 10.1080/15027570.2020.1778880.

Tabullo, A. J., Navas Jiménez, V. A. and Silvana García, C. (2018) 'Associations between fiction reading, trait empathy and theory of mind ability', *Int. j. psychol. psychol. ther. (Ed. impr.)*, pp. 357–370.

Tartakover, S 2013, *Cultural perspectives in school communities: an exploration and representation of cultural identity in pre-service teachers*. PhD thesis, Victoria University. Official URL: https://vimeo.com/132886888

Tashmatova, M. A. (2021) 'the Importance of Intercultural Communicative Competence', *Current Research Journal of Philological Sciences*, 02(06), pp. 73–79. doi: 10.37547/philological-crjps-02-06-15.

Teel, K. M., & Obidah, J. E. (Eds.). (2008). Building racial and cultural competence in the classroom: Strategies from urban educators. New York, NY: Teachers College Press

Tettegah, S. and Anderson, C. J. (2007) 'Pre-service teachers' empathy and cognitions: Statistical analysis of text data by graphical models', *Contemporary Educational Psychology*, 32(1), pp. 48–82. doi: 10.1016/j.cedpsych.2006.10.010.

Tettegah, S. Y. (2005) 'Technology, narratives, vignettes, and the intercultural and cross-cultural teaching portal', *Urban Education*, 40(4), pp. 368–393. doi: 10.1177/0042085905276376.

Thomas Casedy & Berry Robert (2019) 'EDUCATION MATHMATICS', *Journal of Mathematics Education*, 10(1). Available at: https://www.researchgate.net/profile/Mailizar_Mailizar/publication/275967933_HOW_EQUALITY_AND_INEQUALITY_OF_WHOLE_NUMBERS_ARE_INTRODUCED_IN_CHINA_INDONESIA_AND_SAUDI_ARABIAPRIMARY_SCHOOL_TEXTBOOKS/links/554c9d7e0cf29752ee7f1fa6.pdf#page=314.

Trivoli (1996) 'trivoli.pdf'.

Tzanakis, M 2011 'Bourdieu's Social Reproduction'. *Thesis and The Role of Cultural Capital in Educational Attainment*: A Critical Review of Key Empirical Studies *Vol. 11, No. 1, 2011, pp. 76-90*

van Werven, I. M. *et al.* (2021) 'Global teaching competencies in primary education', *Compare*, 53(1), pp. 37–54. doi: 10.1080/03057925.2020.1869520.

Vaughn, S. W. and Johnson, K. A. (2021a) 'Ethnocultural empathy and diversity training: the case of campus policing', *Police Practice and Research*, 22(1), pp. 460–474. doi: 10.1080/15614263.2020.1716753.

Vaughn, S. W. and Johnson, K. A. (2021b) 'Ethnocultural empathy and diversity training: the case of campus policing', *Police Practice and Research*, 22(1), pp. 460–474. doi: 10.1080/15614263.2020.1716753.

Vegas, E. and Ganimian, A. J. (2011) 'What Are the Teacher Policies of Top-Performing and Rapidly-Improving School Systems? - 08-09-11 - FINAL'.

Vegh, J. and Nguyen Luu, L. A. (2019) 'Intercultural Competence Developmental Models – Theory and Practice Through Comparative Analysis', *PEOPLE: International Journal of Social Sciences*, 4(3), pp. 882–901. doi: 10.20319/pijss.2019.43.882901.

Villegas, M., Neugebauer, S. R., & Venegas, K. R. (Eds.) 2008, *Indigenous knowledge and education: Sites of struggle, strength, and survivance*. Harvard Educational Review Reprint Series No. 44. Cambridge, MA: Harvard Education Press.

Vincent, S. K. and Torres, R. M. (2015) 'Multicultural Competence: A Case Study of Teachers and their Student Perceptions', *Journal of Agricultural Education*, 56(2), pp. 64–75. doi: 10.5032/jae.2015.02064.

Vinson, T. S. and Neimeyer, G. J. (2003) 'The Relationship between Racial Identity Development and Multicultural Counseling Competency: A Second Look', *Journal of Multicultural Counseling and Development*, 31(4), pp. 262–277. doi: 10.1002/j.2161-1912.2003.tb00354.x.

Vollet, J. W., Kindermann, T. A. and Skinner, E. A. (2017) 'In peer matters, teachers matter: Peer group influences on students' engagement depend on teacher involvement', *Journal of Educational Psychology*, 109(5), pp. 635–652. doi: 10.1037/edu0000172.

Vygotsky, L. S. 1934, *Mind in society*. Translated by V. John-Steiner and E. Souberman in 1978. Cambridge, MA: Harvard University Press

Walker, V. L. *et al.* (2022) 'Preservice Teachers' Preparation in Communication Instruction for Students with Extensive Support Needs', *Research and Practice for Persons with Severe Disabilities*, 47(1), pp. 57–64. doi: 10.1177/15407969221074720.

Wang, Y. (2013) *Education policy reform trends in G20 members*, *Education Policy Reform Trends in G20 Members*. doi: 10.1007/978-3-642-38931-3.

Wang, Y. W. *et al.* (2003) 'The Scale of Ethnocultural Empathy: Development, validation, and reliability', *Journal of Counseling Psychology*, 50(2), pp. 221–234. doi: 10.1037/0022-0167.50.2.221.

Warren, C. A. (2013) 'The Utility of Empathy for White Female Teachers ' Culturally Responsive Interactions with Black Male Students', 3(3), pp. 175–200.

Warren, C. A. (2014) 'Towards a pedagogy for the application of empathy in culturally diverse classrooms', *Urban Review*, 46(3), pp. 395–419. doi: 10.1007/s11256-013-0262-5.

Warren, C. A. (2015) 'Scale of teacher empathy for African American males (S-TEAAM): Measuring teacher conceptions and the application of empathy in multicultural classroom settings', *Journal of Negro Education*, 84(2), pp. 154–174. doi: 10.7709/jnegroeducation.84.2.0154.

Warren, C. A. (2018) 'Empathy, Teacher Dispositions, and Preparation for Culturally Responsive Pedagogy', *Journal of Teacher Education*, 69(2), pp. 169–183. doi: 10.1177/0022487117712487.

Wawire, B. A. (2021) 'Promoting effective early grade reading: the case study of primary teachers' preparation programmes in Kenya', *Curriculum Journal*, 32(2), pp. 247–268. doi: 10.1002/curj.69.

Weinstein, S. C., Tomlinson-Clarke S., & Curran, M 2004, 'Toward a conception of culturally responsive classroom management', In: *Journal of Teacher Education,* no. 55, pp. 25-38.

Weitkämper, F. (2022) 'Un/Doing authority and social inequality: understanding mutual vulnerability in pupil-teacher relations and challenging situations', *Educational Review*, 0(0), pp. 1–17. doi: 10.1080/00131911.2022.2134311.

References

Wilhelmsen, T. et al. (2022) 'Teachers' competence promote close relationships to children with externalising problems and conflictual relationships', *Educational Psychology*, 42(6), pp. 673–693. doi: 10.1080/01443410.2022.2059653.

Wonacott, M. E. 2001, 'Postmodernism: Yes, no or maybe? Myths and realities Coloumus, Ohio ERIC Clearinghouse on Adult, Career and Vocational Edcation'. No. 15.

Yang, R. and Gao, C. Y. (2020) 'Rethinking Cultural Competence Education in the Global Era: Insights from Fei Xiaotong's Theory of Cultural Self-Awareness', *Frontiers of Education in China*, 15(4), pp. 539–563. doi: 10.1007/s11516-020-0026-4.

Yared, H., Grové, C. and Chapman, D. (2020) *How does race play out in schools? A scoping review and thematic analysis of racial issues in Australian schools*, *Social Psychology of Education*. Springer Netherlands. doi: 10.1007/s11218-020-09589-5.

Yousaf, M. et al. (2022) 'A cross-cultural comparison of ethnocentrism and the intercultural willingness to communicate between two collectivistic cultures', *Scientific Reports*, 12(1), pp. 1–13. doi: 10.1038/s41598-022-21179-3.

Yuan, H. (2017) 'Preparing Teachers for Diversity: A Literature Review and Implications from Community-Based Teacher Education', *Higher Education Studies*, 8(1), p. 9. doi: 10.5539/hes.v8n1p9.

Yuval-davis, N. (1999) 'What is "transversal politics"?', (12), pp. 94–98.

Zaki, J., Bolger, N. and Ochsner, K. (2009) 'Unpacking the Informational Bases of Empathic Accuracy', *Emotion*, 9(4), pp. 478–487. doi: 10.1037/a0016551.

Zembylas, M. and Papamichael, E. (2017) 'Pedagogies of discomfort and empathy in multicultural teacher education', *Intercultural Education*, 28(1), pp. 1-19. doi: 10.1080/14675986.2017.1288448.

Zhu, H. (2011) 'From Intercultural Awareness to Intercultural Empathy', *English Language Teaching*, 4(1), p. 116. doi: 10.5539/elt.v4n1p116.

Ziv, I., Golbez, N. and Shapira, N. (2020) 'Parental sense of competence, resilience, and empathy in relation fathers' responses to children's negative emotions in the context of everyday paternal childrearing decisions', *Cogent Psychology*, 7(1), pp. 1-30. doi: 10.1080/23311908.2020.1794681.

Zubrick, S. R., Silburn, S. R., De Maio, J. A., Shepherd, C., Griffin, J. A., Dalby, R. B., Mitrou, F. G., Lawrence, D. M., Hayward, C., Pearson, G., Milroy, H., Milroy, J. & Cox, A 2006 *Improving the educational experiences of Aboriginal children and young people*. Perth, WA.

www.ingramcontent.com/pod-product-compliance
Lightning Source LLC
Chambersburg PA
CBHW041317110526
44591CB00021B/2811